Geoffrey Parrinder is Professor of the Comparative Study of Religions in the University of London. After ordination he spent twenty years teaching in West Africa, and studying African religions in his spare time, before becoming the founder member of the Department of Religious Studies in the University College of Ibadan, Nigeria. He has travelled widely in Africa, India, Pakistan, Ceylon, Burma, Israel, Jordan, and Turkey and held lecturing appointments in Australia, India, America and at Oxford. He is the author of many books on world religions.

ASIAN RELIGIONS

Geoffrey Parrinder

SHELDON PRESS
LONDON

First published as *An Introduction to Asian Religions* in 1957
Reprinted 1958, 1962, 1968 by SPCK

Published in 1975 by Sheldon Press
Marylebone Road, London NW1 4DU

Printed in Great Britain by
William Clowes & Sons, Limited
London, Beccles and Colchester

ISBN 0 85969 045 8

Contents

1

Introductory

THIS introduction to Asian religions aims at presenting the main facts about the living and literary non-Christian religions, for those who have no previous knowledge of these religions. There are many who look in curiosity at the great religions of Asia and seek a simple and up-to-date guide to their study.

This book discusses the living religious systems of Asia. It does not consider dead religions, such as those of ancient Mesopotamia, or even Zoroastrianism except for a brief mention of the few modern descendants of this religion in the Parsi community. Of the living religions, short historical backgrounds are given, with some account of their scriptures and religious life, and then an attempt is made to indicate something of the position of these religions under modern conditions.

The literary religions are those discussed. The many remnants of primitive religion that are to be found in Asia, as in other continents, will only be referred to incidentally. Some account will be taken, however, of the findings of modern archaeology. The religious literature of Asia is vast, greater than that of any other continent, and going back in origin some 3,000 years. Only very brief quotations can be given from these innumerable scriptures, but typical passages will be quoted as an incentive to further study. Suggestions will also be made of cheap and reliable selections from some of the most important books, that may be obtained for further reading.

I

Only the non-Christian religions are dealt with here. Christianity sprang from western Asia, but it has developed largely outside Asia. It is assumed that the educated reader of English, whether European, African, or American, will already know a good deal more about Christianity than could be put into a short introduction to Asian religions. But mention will be made of important Christian missions to some Asian lands. Indirect Christian influence may also be seen in some modern Asian religious movements, and in the translation of some of their scriptures into European languages.

Islam (or Muhammadanism) is an Asian religion which has spread eastwards as far as China, and westwards across Africa and even into Europe. Islam is nearer to European ways of thought than other Asian religions, and its roots draw some life from Judaism and Christianity. For this reason we shall treat of Islam first, and not at the end as has been the practice in some introductions of this kind.

This book seeks to be factual and impartial. This is important in two ways. On the one hand, there are those who are only interested in Indian or Chinese religions because of their supposed magical contents. This book is not for them. It tries to give a fair and rounded picture of religion, not magic. A book on Christianity would not need to give place to alchemy or astrology.

On the other hand, there are those who are suspicious of any kind of comparison of religious systems. There was an old type of Christian argument which sought to display the excellencies of its own faith, to the discredit of others. This sort of apologetic is suspect in many places to-day. Here at least we shall be content to state the facts as fairly as possible, and leave the reader to draw his own conclusions. The Christian will know how to make his own comparisons. The non-Christian will not be attracted by biased propaganda.

For this reason also, the best will be brought out wherever possible, but without shirking a glimpse of lower forms. All religions have unworthy followers and strange sects, but all would wish to be judged by their best.

A further error needs to be guarded against, however. That

is the perverted prejudice of the man who sees all the good in other religions, and little or none in his own. There is the strange spectacle to be seen to-day of some European intellectuals who speak in unqualified admiration of the Indian Vedanta, for example, but in shrill criticism of the Bible. One cannot but feel distrust for exaggerated reactions of this kind.

Somewhat similar has been the attitude of certain colonial officials, nominally Christian, who have opposed Christianity in predominantly Muslim lands (e.g. still in British Somaliland). This has often been done under the pretence that all religions are the same. No self-respecting Muslim believes that all religions are the same, nor does he fail to propagate his religion wherever he may go.

It has been said that the religious thought of our time suffers from the four heresies of Darwinism, Frazerism, Freudism, and Marxism. These labels, not altogether fair to the original writers to whose names the -isms are attached, mean briefly as follows. Darwinism, from Charles Darwin the naturalist, indicates the theory that human life has developed from the animal level. In the religious sphere, it suggests that all religions will develop in the same way if they are only left alone. This takes no account of the unexpected emergence of great religious teachers, or of acts of divine grace and special revelation. It would not permit the work of the missionaries of Christianity, Islam, and Buddhism.

Frazerism, following on Sir James Frazer's great series of books *The Golden Bough*, means the indiscriminate collection of examples of all types of religious and magical practice, lumping them under various heads, and concluding that "all religions are of equal value". This is no more sensible than to maintain that all men have equal abilities.

Freudism, from Sigmund Freud the Austrian psychologist, is taken as the dismissing of all religion as a fallacy, a projection of human desires. This is not only against the great mass of human religious experiences and scriptures, and against the trend of all human history, but in recent years it has been seen clearly that men must have a faith to live

3

by (even degraded forms of faith such as Fascism and Nazism).

Marxism, from Karl Marx the German communist, calls religion the opiate of the masses, a drug to keep men under subjection. All that men need, it says, is better pay, more food, and bigger houses. But the fact that Communism itself has become almost a religion, with the writings of Marx as its scriptures, shows plainly enough that man does not live by bread alone.

None of these heresies explains the great diversity of the religions of the world. They do not explain the continuing interest in religion which is apparent in the modern world which, with all its scientific knowledge and economic betterment, is yet hungry for the things of the soul. Nor do these heresies explain, or even admit, the facts of revelations of God. Indeed they try to explain away religion without reference to God; which is absurd and irrational.

Here, then, we shall endeavour to divest ourselves of the anti-religious bias of some writers of our time. That we believe in the value and genuineness of some of the religious experiences of followers of the noblest Asian religions cannot be denied. To be fair we must recognize their worth. This, after all, is the traditional catholic and Christian position. God has not left himself without witness, "as certain even of your own poets have said, For we also are his offspring".

4

2

Islam

ISLAM is the religion founded by the Arabian prophet Muhammad (formerly miscalled Mahomet). The name Islam means surrender, or resignation, to the will of God. From the same verbal root comes the name Muslim (or Moslem; Musulman in Persia) given to the one who has surrendered to or received the religion. A Muslim is one who has given himself exclusively to God, a monotheist, a worshipper of the one God as revealed by Muhammad.

Muslims use the name Islam for their religion, and they do not like the title Muhammadan given to them by Christians. They do not worship Muhammad, but they believe that he was the last and greatest Apostle of God, whose revelation outdates all others.

ARABIA BEFORE MUHAMMAD

Islam is a late-comer among the world's religions. It is much younger than Buddhism and Christianity and, like them, it is a reformation of older religious beliefs, with new material added, and made into a world-religion.

Mecca and Medina, the two towns where Muhammad lived, are on the western edge of central Arabia, surrounded by desert or steppe, and closely linked with nomadic peoples. These towns were important stages in the international routes that led from Abyssinia to Syria and Mesopotamia. Many caravans passed through them, and so the townsmen were traders and middlemen. They were not lost in isolation but were on the highways of life.

In Mecca groups within the community were constantly struggling for power. The tribe of Quraysh (Koreish) held the town and different clans jostled for supremacy. Muhammad belonged to a well-established but poor family within the town.

Mecca was a religious centre before the time of Muhammad. Its chief holy place was the Kabah (cube), a cube-like stone building, twelve yards long, ten broad, and fifteen high. In the south-east corner of the Kabah is the Black Stone, about seven inches in diameter. The tribes from the desert flocked to Mecca every year during the month of pilgrimage, and brought considerable gain to the townsfolk. The pilgrims went round the Kabah and kissed the Black Stone, as they do still. There were other temples and a few other Kabahs elsewhere in Arabia.

Possibly the name Allah was used to indicate the chief God of the Kabah before Muhammad's time. The word Allah is from al-ilah, "the god", but used of "the supreme God". But other gods were also worshipped by the Arabs. The Quran (Koran) mentions three goddesses, Al-Lat, Al-Uzza, and Al-Manat, representing the Sun, the planet Venus, and Fortune. The Meccans called these goddesses daughters of Allah.

Many other spirits were believed in; the spirits of wells, springs, rocks, and trees. Blood sacrifices were made at sacred stones and bonds were thus established between gods and men. Altogether it is not unlike the picture of Canaan in the early parts of the Old Testament.

Considerable importance attaches to the presence of Jews and Christians in Arabia, since Muhammad refers to both and gives versions of stories from the Bible. There were large colonies of Jews who had migrated to Arabia from Palestine at different periods, especially during the Roman persecutions at the beginning of our era. It is estimated that about half the population of Medina was Jewish, both traders and agriculturists, and there were a few of them in Mecca also.

Christianity was strong in the surrounding empires of Abyssinia, Byzantium, and Persia. There were some Christian

6

communities in Arabia, and it is said that some Christian paintings decorated the interior walls of the Kabah. Unhappily the Christians were divided into rival sects. Many of them had adopted practices which were later reflected in Islam. Some taught women to be veiled out of doors; most Christians turned to the east in prayer; and fanciful apocryphal stories were told about Jesus and sacred history, some of which are later told in the Quran.

Both Jews and Christians were "people of a Book", and both believed in one God. These prepared the way for Islam.

MUHAMMAD

Muhammad was born about the year A.D. 570. This year is called the Year of the Elephant, in which an Abyssinian army with elephants came unsuccessfully against Mecca.

Muhammad's father, Abd Allah, had died before the child was born, and his mother also died six years later. He came under the charge of his uncle Abu Talib and travelled with him to Syria, and also took part in some of the tribal skirmishes. Stories are told of angelic beings who visited Muhammad in boyhood and took a black clot out of his heart. A Christian monk is also reported to have seen the seal of prophecy between Muhammad's shoulders.

When Muhammad was twenty-five years old he married a wealthy widow called Khadijah. He had already acted as her agent on a trade mission to Damascus and she was impressed by his character and ability. Khadijah was forty at this time, but she bore Muhammad six children, two boys who died in infancy and four daughters of whom Fatima is memorable for her marriage to Ali the fourth Caliph (*Khalifah*, successor of Muhammad), in whose line the Prophet's successors are revered. Khadijah was a great help to Muhammad. She encouraged him in his prophecy, and as long as she lived he took no other wife.

Not until he was forty years old did the call to prophecy come to Muhammad. He had already become fond of solitude and used to retire to caves in the mountains to pray and meditate. We are told that one night an angel appeared to him and said: "O Muhammad, I am Gabriel, and thou art the messenger of God." Then Gabriel commanded him, "Recite." When Muhammad asked what to recite, he was told:

> "Recite in the name of thy Lord who created,
> Created man from clots of blood.
> Recite. For thy Lord is the most beneficent,
> Who hath taught the use of the pen,
> Hath taught man that which he knoweth not."[1]

This is Surah (chapter) 96 of the Quran, but it seems to have been the first to be revealed. The name Quran for the holy book of Islam comes from a root which means "recite" or "address". It is a dogma that Muhammad could neither read nor write, but that all the Quran was recited by him as he received it from Gabriel.

After his vision Muhammad, like some other religious visionaries, was filled with terror and contemplated suicide. But Khadijah comforted him, and Gabriel again appeared to call him, saying, "Thou art the Prophet of God."

It used to be fashionable for critics of Islam to call Muhammad an epileptic, but there is no ground for this. Muhammad was a prophet (nabi) comparable to Elijah or Amos. Such men are not normal, but that does not mean to say that they are diseased. Muhammad had a great deal of practical wisdom, as well as spiritual insight, and he was in turn a competent trader, a wary general, and a thoughtful administrator.

There followed a gap in the visions, and then they began again. With that, Muhammad began to recount them to other people. He had been told to arise and warn men of the coming Judgement.

> "O thou, enwrapped in thy mantle!
> Arise and warn!
> Thy Lord—magnify him!
> Thy raiment—purify it!

[1] The Koran, translated by J. M. Rodwell, Surah 96.

The abomination—flee it!
And bestow not favours that thou mayest
    receive again with increase;
And for thy Lord wait thou patiently.
For when there shall be a trump on the trumpet,
That shall be a distressful day,
A day, to the Infidels, devoid of ease."[1]

A small following of disciples began to attach themselves to Muhammad. Khadijah was the first to believe in his message, and then small numbers of mainly young and poor men. When Abu Bakr, an important man and later the first Caliph, joined the movement it was greatly strengthened.

With the growth of the movement, and the knowledge of its meetings for community prayer, opposition began from the Meccans. They saw a threat to their position and wealth as guardians of an important sanctuary of the gods. Many are said to have listened to him until he denounced their idols, and then they turned back and left him. Muhammad was accused of sorcery and fraud, and these debates are reflected in the Quran.

Some hundreds of his followers took refuge in Christian Abyssinia. Muhammad remained in Mecca, protected by his uncle, but before long both the latter and the faithful Khadijah died (about A.D. 619). One consolation was the conversion of Umar (Omar), who later became the second Caliph and a great leader. Muhammad now married a widow called Sauda, and Ayesha the daughter of his friend Abu Bakr.

A change from the persecution of Mecca came with the visit of pilgrims from the town of Medina (earlier called Yathrib and renamed Medina "the city" of Muhammad). Six of these pilgrims were converted to Muhammad's message and went home as missionaries of his doctrine. The next year twelve came, and the following year seventy-five Medinans accepted Islam. This aroused the anger of the Meccans and they revived persecution so fiercely that

[1] Surah 74.

9

Muhammad ordered his disciples to migrate to Medina, 220 miles to the north. Finally he followed them himself, by a devious route. This is the famous Hijrah (Hegira), migration, which marks the beginning of the Muslim era and from which its years are dated. It was in A.D. 622.

Medina at that time had been rent by tribal strife, and Muhammad was able to stabilize the situation. He was leader of an important religious community and he set to work to unify it, and make his religion that social and political organism that it has been ever since. He tried first of all to win over the Medinan Jews, by ordering his disciples to turn in prayer towards Jerusalem. But the Jews were critical of him and ridiculed his knowledge of scripture. So the Muslims turned to Mecca for prayer, as always since. Islam thus became truly Arabian, though biblical links were not broken since the Kabah is said to have been built by Abraham.

Muhammad now had two aims: to convert all Arabia to Islam and purify the Kabah from idols, and to destroy the Jewish communities. He preached the duty of Holy War (*jihad*), and began by attacking a caravan from Mecca. After this success he fought about a thousand Meccans at a place called Badr and routed them with three hundred Muslims. Then, having attracted other Arabs to his victories, he turned against the Jews, killing some and exiling others after taking their possessions. So the emigrant community at Medina was greatly enriched.

In 625 the Meccans attacked Medina with three thousand men. Muhammad met them at Uhud, and was defeated. This was a blow to the morale of his troops, but he himself, though wounded, defied the Meccans. Paradise was promised to those Muslim warriors who died fighting for the faith. A still larger army from Mecca had to withdraw before the strong forces of Medina.

Many desert tribes now joined Muhammad or were subdued by him, and this growing strength at last forced the Meccans to make a truce. Muhammad claimed the right to enter Mecca as a pilgrim, and this was granted. In 630 the Meccans broke the truce by attacking a tribe under

Muhammad's protection. He immediately marched on Mecca with ten thousand men and took it after only small opposition. He went to the Kabah fully armed, touched the Black Stone with his staff and called out "God is great" (*Allahu akbar*), which was echoed by his army. He then destroyed the idols and told the multitude that the days of paganism were over and that Allah was sole God, and that blood-vengeance and usury must be abolished. He was merciful to his old enemies and pardoned many. Then he returned to Medina.

Muhammad died in A.D. 632, only ten years after the Hijrah and two years after his conquest of Mecca. He had suffered from abdominal trouble for some time. In 632 he contracted a serious fever. As he became worse he was tended by his favourite wife, Ayesha. He attempted to go to the mosque but Abu Bakr had to lead prayers. The fever increased in violence and at last the Prophet died, his head in Ayesha's lap, and murmuring, "No, the friend, the highest in Paradise."

THE QURAN

The Quran is not an easy book to read. Thomas Carlyle called it "as toilsome reading as I ever undertook". This is certainly the impression that one gets in a simple translation where, as in Arabic, some of the longest and most involved chapters come first. For this reason the reader of English is advised to start with a version that puts the shorter and earlier chapters first. Rodwell's translation in the Everyman's Library, though old, is still one of the easiest versions.

The Quran is divided into 114 chapters, called surahs. Each surah has a title taken from some word that occurs in the text. Each line is rhymed (in Arabic), and the whole book is composed in a sort of rhymed prose, or verses with rhyme but no metre or fixed length. The rhyme is lost of course in translation.

The first surah is short. It is a prayer which opens the book and is called "The Opening" (*Fatihah*). It is headed with the formula (the *Bismillah*, "In the name of God") that stands over nearly every surah: "In the Name of God, the Compassionate, the Merciful." Then the first surah begins:

> Praise be to God, Lord of the worlds,
> The compassionate, the merciful.
> King on the Day of Judgement.
> Thee only do we worship, and to thee do we cry
>   for help.
> Guide thou us on the straight path,
> The path of those to whom thou hast been gracious,
> With whom thou art not angry, and who go not
>   astray.

This surah is recited at all the daily prayers and on many other occasions, and is concluded by Amen. It is often followed by surah 112:

> Say, He is God alone:
> God the eternal.
> He begetteth not, and is not begotten,
> And there is none like unto him.[1]

It is thought that the shorter surahs are, for the most part, the early ones and date from the first Meccan period, together with passages from some of the other surahs. The later and Medinan surahs are mostly longer and more prosy, dealing with the complex situation of social life. They are less in the nature of urgent prophetic messages and more like regulations or debates.

Several themes of Muhammad's teaching will already be observable. God's might in creation is clear in the surah of the call to prophecy (surah 96): "the Lord who created man from clotted blood". It is a Muslim tradition that all mankind is created from clots of blood, with the exception of Adam, Eve, and Jesus.

God is not only a powerful creator, but he is the Merciful, the Compassionate. He is also the King or the "Wielder" of the Day of Judgement. Belief in the Judgement is prominent in the early surahs, but without the lurid details that are

[1] Rodwell, op. cit.

found at a later date. In surah 47 hell-fire is described as draughts of boiling water forced on the damned, while the faithful drink rivers of wine. This is like some early Christian apocalypses. There appear also the purified female companions (houris), and Satan, and the Jinn, the eerie spirits by which the Arabs believed themselves to be surrounded.

The unity of God is, of course, the great message that runs through Muhammad's words and work from start to finish. God alone is creator. The false gods "have created nothing, but are themselves created", they "will not create a fly, even if they join together to do it" (surahs 25 and 22). The words we quoted earlier, "There is none like unto him", are directed against the gods of the Arab people and perhaps also against the Trinity.

Muhammad is regarded as the Apostle or Messenger (*rasul*) of Allah. He is filled with a passionate conviction of his divine call and task. He has to proclaim the unity of God to the Arab people. At first he seems to have thought that one messenger was sent to each people with a book, Moses to the Jews with the Law, Jesus to the Christians with the Gospel. So Muhammad would bring his book, the Quran, to the Arabs who would thus become a people of a book. Later came the knowledge that there had been numbers of messengers, and that Abraham was a prophet to the heathen before the Lawbook was given. Abraham being claimed as ancestor of the Arabs, it became Muhammad's task to call the Arabs back to their early monotheism. But since he believed both Jews and Christians to have fallen away from the teaching of their founders, it was Muhammad's vocation to be "a reminder to the world".

In the narrative parts of the Quran there are many references to stories from the Bible, especially the Old Testament. The creation in six days is often mentioned, and the fall of Adam. Many of the early Old Testament figures appear, with special fondness for Abraham as founder of the Arab religion and reputed builder of the Kabah, and Solomon as a master of winds and jinn. It is clear that Muhammad had not read the Old Testament, for there are many differences of detail, and

13

he probably derived his information from Jews of whom he inquired about important biblical personages.

It is even more certain that Muhammad had no direct knowledge of the New Testament. He teaches the Virgin Birth of Jesus, "We sent our spirit to Mary"; the Last Supper is understood as "a furnished table sent down out of heaven" (surah 5); and the Crucifixion is said to have been only in appearance, "they crucified him not, but they had only his likeness . . . but God took him up to himself" (surah 4). Some of these distortions of the Gospel were current among heretical Christian sects, such as the Docetists who believed that Jesus appeared only and could not die. Muhammad did not understand the doctrine of the Trinity, thinking it included Mary instead of the Holy Spirit. He quotes Jesus as refusing that men should "take me and my mother as two Gods, beside God" (surah 5).

Although Muhammad learnt much from the Jews and something from Christians, yet he broke with the Jews at Medina and later with the Christians as well. Nevertheless Jesus has been honoured in Islam down the ages, and the Peoples of the Book are always preferred above idolaters.

The Quran is said to have been written first on "pieces of paper, stones, palm-leaves, shoulder-blades, ribs, bits of leather, and the hearts of men". It is said that a year or more after Muhammad's death many of those who had heard and memorized parts of it were killed and Abu Bakr ordered Zaid, who had been a secretary to the Prophet, to collect all the material that he could. Later Uthman had an authoritative text prepared so that variants could not be quoted to upset the authority of the official text.

It seems that Muhammad employed a number of people to write down his words. It is believed by Muslims that the revelations were given to him by Gabriel, and that Muhammad recited them to the people. The official doctrine of Islam is that the Quran is eternal, it is the uncreated Word of God, the speech of Allah, revealed to the Prophet, recited by the tongues, preserved in the memories, and written in the copies.

Five times a day, throughout the Muslim world, the faithful are called to prayer by the cry: "God is great. I testify that there is no God but Allah. I testify that Muhammad is the Apostle of God" (*Allahu akbar. La ilaha illa 'llahu. Muhammad rasulu 'llah*).

Wherever he is the pious Muslim will unroll his mat, wash himself ritually, and pray facing in the direction of Mecca. If he can go to the mosque he will do so. Women normally pray at home.

Prayer is one of the essential duties, the pillars of Islam. It consists of a fixed number of bowings and prostrations, recitation of the first surah of the Quran, and other passages. On Friday, the sacred day, the noontide congregational prayer is enjoined on all males. Work is suspended then, but not throughout the day.

A mosque (place of prostration) is a building like a church, but it has no images, paintings, or decoration except for Arabic lettering on the walls. There is a central niche which shows the direction of Mecca, a pulpit, and usually a lectern. There are no pews, but mats on the floor. No music is used in worship, and there is no collection. The preacher speaks in the vernacular, quoting from the Quran in Arabic and generally translating afterwards.

Almsgiving is another duty of all Muslims, as a mark of piety. According to Muslim law one-fortieth of the income should be given to the poor. This tends to encourage professional beggars, but that is almost inevitable in countries where there are few social services.

Fasting is enjoined also, originally from the practice of Jews and Christians. During the month of Ramadan, the ninth month of the lunar year, no food or drink must pass the lips between sunrise and sunset. It is not a total fast, because eating can be done at night, but the long day's abstinence can be very trying in hot climates. The fast of Ramadan is strictly observed, though exceptions are made for children, the sick, and travellers. Wine and pork are forbidden to Muslims at all times.

Pilgrimage to Mecca is a duty at least once in a lifetime, if one is in good health and can afford the expense. We have seen that Mecca was a place of pilgrimage long before Islam, and the Muslim ritual includes the ancient practice of going round the Kabah seven times and kissing the Black Stone. Other places are to be visited, especially the Prophet's tomb at Medina.

Prayer, fasting, almsgiving, pilgrimage, and the profession of faith in Allah and his Apostle, these make up the five Pillars of Faith.

An attempt was made to add the Holy War (*jihad*) as a sixth pillar of religion. The Quran gave its sanction to such war against unbelievers. Clearly this was meant for Arabia in the Prophet's day. Later it was extended to the Muslim wars of conquest in Asia, Africa, and Europe. But the fanaticism of extremists led to a rejection of this exaltation of Jihad. A more spiritual meaning was given to the term. One writer said, "The holy war has ten parts, one of fighting the enemy of Islam, nine of fighting the self." To-day it is explained that the real war is against sin.

SOCIAL CUSTOMS AND BELIEFS

Islam claims to be a brotherhood that unites its followers. All men are the slaves of God and so are equal in his sight. This does not mean that there are no social divisions, between rich and poor, freemen and slaves, men and women. But in the mosque men bow together before the one God of all. Women, however, rarely join in public worship.

In Muslim law God is the head of the state, and the Caliphs were his deputies. Judges were appointed in every town who considered lawsuits in their own houses or in the mosques. Judges follow one of the four schools of law (called after their founders): Maliki in Upper Egypt and North and West Africa; Shafii in Lower Egypt and parts of Arabia and East Africa; Hanbali in Wahhabi Arabia; Hanafi in most of Asia.

In addition to matters of faith and ritual, the Quran

contains a great deal of ethical and legal teaching. Muhammad found it necessary to lay down or begin to codify regulations for inheritance, dowries, divorce, and the guardianship of orphans. He ordered an end of the blood-feud that so ravaged Arab clans, and made penalties for murder, theft, fraud, perjury, and slander. These are all expanded in the later tradition (*sunna*).

Muslim ethics, like the Greek, show the importance of the middle way between extremes. They are particularly social: hospitality is one of the greatest virtues, to fulfil which a man would make any effort. Unbelief is the greatest sin, followed by murder, adultery, and the like. Blood revenge, a life for a life, is permitted as in the Mosaic law, but not beyond one life, thus forbidding a tribal feud.

A great deal is said in the Quran about women. As among the Hebrews, the primary aim of marriage is regarded as the begetting of children. Partly for this reason polygamy is allowed up to four wives, with an unlimited number of concubines. Muhammad himself had ten wives, yet no son survived him. He laid down this rule for his followers: "Of women who seem good in your eyes, marry but two, or three, or four; and if ye still fear that ye shall not act equitably, then one only" (surah 4). Many millions of Muslims to-day have only one wife each, and some modern teachers declare that monogamy is binding on all Muslims as is shown by the last clause of the verse quoted above, since one cannot "act equitably" to more than one wife.

Divorce is easy for men, but not for women. On pronouncing a traditional formula the divorce is attained, but the man can take the woman back if he changes his mind. A charge of adultery needs to be supported by four witnesses, and as this evidence is almost impossible to obtain the husband swears five times that he is speaking the truth and the marriage is annulled.

A Muslim can marry a Jewess or a Christian but not a pagan, whereas a Muslim woman must marry a Muslim. If her husband changes his religion the marriage is dissolved. Circumcision was already practised by the Arabs, and

Muhammad adopted it as part of the religion of Abraham. Female circumcision is practised in some places.

Slavery was recognized by Muhammad as an institution, but the good treatment of slaves was prescribed. It was quite different from the mass slavery of the American plantations. While slaves worked in Muslim houses or gardens they were not exploited on a large scale. Slaves were family retainers and were often freed at the death of their masters. Many slaves rose to high position or influence. The Mamlukes of Egypt rose from slavery to become rulers of the country, and at first no one could occupy the throne if he had not been a slave.

Funeral ceremonies among Muslims follow ancient customs in the main. Burial is usually the same day or the following day in hot countries. The body is not usually taken to the mosque, but short prayers are said over it and it is carried on an open bier to the cemetery. Coffins are used in some parts to-day, but the body is buried in its shroud and the coffin is used again for other burials. The corpse is laid on the right side, facing Mecca, and often in a niche so that the earth does not fall on it. The top of the grave is supposed to be levelled with the ground, but there are often elaborate tombstones, with fantastic designs and Arabic texts. Women visit the grave each Friday for forty days after the funeral, taking a palm branch to put on the grave and cakes to give to the poor.

The tombs of saints are often very elaborate and a mosque with a dome usually indicates that it is also a tomb. Saint-worship is widespread in Muslim lands, perhaps as a relief to the stern monotheism of a distant monarchical God. Some saints are revered throughout the Muslim world, and are called upon for help in any time of need. Others are of local fame only, and where they are associated with wells, trees, rocks, and caves the cult probably incorporates some ancient nature-worship. Saints' tombs are highly respected, and anything left there is inviolate. Saints have their annual birthdays (*mawlid*) and festivals, with prayers, processions, and fairs.

Living saints and holy men (marabouts) are greatly revered. Their blessing and touch has almost magical power. They are appealed to in time of war as arbitrators. They are akin to the members of religious orders which have convents where teaching is given and hospitality is available. Mention of the Sufi mystics will be made later.

There is widespread belief in magic among the ordinary Muslims. Whereas the miracles of saints come from God, the power of magic is believed to come from jinn (good and evil spirits). Solomon is said to have been a great worker of white magic, and he called up jinns to order. Magical talismans and amulets are very common, and verses from the Quran, especially surahs 113 and 114, are much used as protections against witchcraft and the evil eye. Exorcism of those possessed by evil jinn is practised in Egypt and North Africa, by methods said to have come from Central Africa. In this exorcism music, trances, and sacrifice play prominent parts.

There has always been debate in Islam about the use of music. The law forbids it in the mosque, but mystics have used it to induce a state in which they felt able to enter into communion with God. After long argument the theologians admitted the value of music, but hedged its use about with restrictions. The association of wine, women, and song was noted and reprehended. So songs when used must not tend to immorality or irreligion.

Similarly painting and sculpture were forbidden, because of the tendency towards idolatry. The prohibition was often ignored, and Muslim craftsmen in Persia and India, especially, made pictures of animals and men. The prohibition turned the energies of Muslim artists to beauty of line in the architecture of lovely mosques and tombs, and to development of decoration in geometrical forms and in Arabic writing. The Alhambra palace in Granada still stands as a wonderful example of decoration in countless ways without the use of bodily representation, except in the famous Courtyard of the Lions with its twelve stone lion-fountains.

Nowadays, with the introduction of photography and illustrated newspapers in Muslim lands, a relaxation of custom is taking place. Similarly a slackening of the law against usury is allowed for those who wish to draw interest on banking accounts. In contact with the modern world many customs have to be adapted, as others have for long been adapted in India, where Muslims have lived in close contact with the Hindus who delight in sculpture and music.

THE SPREAD OF ISLAM

When Muhammad died in A.D. 632 only Arabia was under Muslim rule, and the Prophet probably never looked for the extension of his religion and rule beyond his own land. Yet only ten years later all Syria, Palestine, Mesopotamia, and Egypt had been brought into the new Muslim Empire. From a religion of the Arab people, Islam was so quickly to become a world-faith.

Muhammad had left no provision for the succession to his leadership, and his father-in-law and friend Abu Bakr was quickly appointed Caliph (*Khalifa*, deputy), to the chagrin of the Medinans and some of the Meccans. Abu Bakr had to take quick action against some of the tribes, who thought that their loyalty to Islam was broken by the death of Muhammad. From this military action his armies turned almost insensibly to attack the lands beyond Arabia.

Abu Bakr died after two years and was succeeded by Umar who had already been the power behind the throne. His chief general was Khalid who led the Arab raiders across to Mesopotamia and then through the desert to Damascus, which he sacked in 634. The Byzantine rulers of Syria and Palestine collected their armies against the Arab invaders, but they met with a crushing defeat and these lands fell easily into Arab hands. Similarly the Persian empire gathered its forces, but they were heavily defeated in 637 and the Arab armies captured the Persian capital of Ctesiphon and occupied all Mesopotamia.

Egypt fell even more easily into Arab hands. A force of ten thousand men captured nearly all Lower Egypt in 640. It must be said that the Egyptians hated their Byzantine Greek rulers, although both were nominally Christian, and they helped the Arab invaders. Similarly in Syria and Mesopotamia it was the welcome of the native population which proved of great help to the Arabs.

The Arabs were hailed as liberators, and their early rule was not oppressive. The ancient fable that the Caliphs destroyed the famous library at Alexandria has long been proved a libel. The Arabs demanded the conversion of idolaters, but other religions were tolerated on payment of a tax. This led many waverers to come over to Islam. But on the whole Jews and Christians thought Arab rule milder than that of Byzantium.

In 644 the Caliph Umar was murdered by a Persian slave. In his place Uthman was elected. It was a bad choice. He was known as a coward, and had been put in as a member of a Meccan ruling family. The Medinans, who had done so much for Muhammad, were furious. Uthman's weakness and favouritism brought out long-smouldering resentments which he did not know how to control. Finally armed rebellion broke out and in 656 Uthman was murdered by fellow-Muslims in Medina.

Ali, cousin and son-in-law of the Prophet, was at once acclaimed as fourth Caliph in Medina. But opposition to him was led by Ayesha, the Prophet's widow, and this caused a schism which has run through the Muslim world. Ali left Medina and led an army against Ayesha's allies and defeated them in the "Battle of the Camel", which ranged round the camel on which Ayesha, "the Mother of the Faithful", was riding. Ali became master of the Muslim empire with the exception of Syria where Muawiya was general. After skirmishes and efforts at arbitration, Ali had to give up hopes of Syria and finally he lost Egypt also to his rival. In 661 Ali was murdered by a fanatic.

Ali's son Hasan gave up the struggle, and resigned his rights to Muawiya who soon became Caliph over the whole empire. Muawiya was the first ruler of the Umayyad dynasty which lasted from A.D. 661 to 750. Later Arab historians refused the title Caliph to these rulers, and called them Kings instead, secular rulers instead of spiritual deputies of the Prophet. True, their capital was moved to Syria, yet the Umayyads were Arabs, and they spread Muslim rule from Europe to India and penetrated into China.

By 705 Arab forces in the east had entered India and soon

occupied Sind. An Arab embassy visited the Chinese court in 713, and helped put down a rebellion there in 755. At the other extreme, in the west, they crossed over from North Africa into Spain in 709 and up into France, where their advance was checked by Charles Martel at the battle of Poitiers in 732.

With the fall of the Umayyads to the Abbasid dynasty in 750, the centre of empire shifted from Syria to Mesopotamia, with Persian influence dominant. A reading of the *Arabian Nights* gives some idea of the society of those days. The Caliph was now more powerful than ever, the "Deputy of God" even more than the Deputy of the Prophet of God. There was a high degree of prosperity and civilization. Yet before long this empire began to break up into smaller units under independent rulers. Egypt came to be ruled by the Fatimid dynasty who built Cairo and made the mosque of Al-Azhar their religious centre. In their prosperity they ruled over North Africa and parts of Europe.

In 827 the Muslims occupied the island of Sicily and threatened Italy and even Rome itself. In Spain the Arab rule was welcomed as preferable to that of the Franks. Culture flourished, poor farmers had lands distributed to them, and many of the rich turned over to Islam. Christians and Jews were protected, but inevitably Arabic came to oust Latin and eventually the Bible had to be translated into Arabic for the use of Spanish Christians. The Franks only slowly re-conquered Spain. At the end of the thirteenth century all Spain, except Granada, was again under Christian rule.

In the thirteenth century Arab civilization was stricken by the Mongol hordes of Jenghiz Khan. He and his successors captured Baghdad and destroyed the Persian power. Later came the Turks who, in 1453, captured Constantinople (Istanbul) where their rulers assumed the title of Caliph. They marched into eastern Europe as far as Vienna, before they were thrown back in 1683.

Under the Turks the Arab world went into stagnation for centuries. In the earlier period Arab and Islamic civilization had preserved culture through the Dark Ages, and the

European scholars of the Middle Ages and the Renaissance owed to them much of their cultural heritage.

SECTS

Like other religions Islam soon split up into many different sects, some of which have disappeared and have little interest for the general modern reader; others have lasted over the centuries and yet others are still appearing. Only a few important ones are mentioned here.

Shia.

This is the great division that separates the followers of Ali from the traditionalists (Sunni). The name Shia means "party, followers", and is used distinctively of the sect of Ali. It will be remembered that when Ali was murdered in 661 his son Hasan gave up his claim to the caliphate. When the first Umayyad Caliph died a younger son of Ali, Husain, came out in rebellion, leaving Medina for Mesopotamia. He was intercepted and slain at a place called Karbala, his followers regarded him as a martyr, and to this day there is a great Passion Play held annually near Baghdad in his memory, and another at Karbala. Some compare Husain's death with that of Jesus.

The Shia sect increased rapidly, and to-day their strongholds are in Mesopotamia, Persia, and Pakistan. The Shia organization is similar to that of Sunni Islam, but they reject the first three Caliphs as usurpers and insist on the exclusive right of the house of Ali, and this offends the Sunni. The Shia preferred the name Imam (leader) for the head of the state, and believed that there were twelve divinely appointed Imams, trust in whom is an article of faith. The last Imam disappeared in A.D. 878 and they await his return as Mahdi (guided one) who will fill the earth with justice. The doctrine of the Mahdi, accepted by some of the Sunni as referring to the return of Christ, has given rise to many pretenders.

Ismailiya.

The Shia soon divided into sects, of which the Ismailiya is one of the most interesting and parent of other offshoots.

They look upon a certain Ismail as the seventh Imam, but unfortunately little is known about him, though his followers consider him as second only to God. The movement became a secret society, one branch of which, the Assassins, has become known in the West because in the time of the Crusades they intoxicated themselves with hashish and went out to murder Christians (hence the name Hashash, Assassin).

The Druzes of Lebanon are another branch of the Ismailiya. The Khoja sect, found mainly in Pakistan, regards the Aga Khan as sacred and pays him tithes; this sect has been affected by some Indian religious ideas.

Wahhabi.

This is a modern movement though reactionary in teaching. It was founded in the eighteenth century by Al-Wahhab who protested against innovations in Islam, especially saint-worship, and the appeal to prophets or angels for intercession. They are very puritanical and forbid the use of gold ornaments, tobacco, music, and even playing chess. The Wahhabi have gained control of most of Arabia, including Mecca and Medina. They have put down amusements and closed eating-houses. However, the exploitation of oil has brought the importation of cars, wireless, and even alcohol and tobacco for strangers, at least.

Ahmadiyya.

This sect arose in India and shows some of the religious mixture of that land. In 1880 the founder Ghulam Ahmad claimed to be both Messiah and Mahdi. Later he claimed to be a manifestation also of the Hindu god Krishna. After his death great reverence was paid to his tomb.

The chief interest of the sect lies in its missionary character. It has sent numerous missionaries to Africa and Europe (cf. the mosque at Woking). But by Sunni Muslims it is regarded as quite heretical.

India has had its effect upon Islam, and other movements have arisen in the past which have sought to reconcile Islam and Hinduism. Some reference will be made to the more important of these when dealing with Indian religion.

It is the mystical side of Islam that most frequently makes a greater appeal to the non-Muslim than the formal worship and the external law. It seems no accident that many of the greatest mystics arose in Persia, a land which, after showing the world the noble religion of Zarathustra, in turn became Christian and Muslim, with Hindu influences also playing upon it.

The name commonly given to the mystics of Islam is Sufi, a word which is said to be derived from *suf*, wool, because like the Christian ascetics they wore undyed woollen clothes. The Sufis are divided into innumerable sects, and differ in dress and customs, but they agree in the necessity of submission to an inspired guide and they teach union with God.

One of the first and greatest Sufis was Rabia, a poor freed female slave of Basra, who died in A.D. 801. The reverence in which Rabia is held shows that mysticism gave women the opportunity of sainthood. There seems to have been more freedom for women in orthodox Islam in the early days than there was later, and the mystics have demonstrated this freedom. They honour the Mother of Jesus, Our Lady Mariam, above all women, above men too, and claim that she reached perfection. Rabia herself was said to be "a second spotless Mary".

Rabia had a long life and uttered bold doctrines. Her faith was based on love to God. At her morning prayer she said:

"O my Joy and my Desire and my Refuge,
My Friend and my Sustainer and my Goal,
Thou art my intimate, and longing for thee
        sustains me.
Were it not for thee, O my Life and my Friend,
How I should have been distraught over the spaces
        of the earth."

Very much like a Spanish Christian she prayed:

> "O my Lord, if I worship thee from fear of Hell, burn me in Hell, and if I worship thee from hope of Paradise, exclude me thence, but if I worship thee for thine own sake then withhold not from me thine Eternal Beauty."

Rabia was seen one day running through the streets carrying fire in one hand and water in the other. She said, "I am going to light a fire in Paradise and pour water on Hell so that the servants of God may see him without any object of hope or motive of fear."

Perhaps her most famous verse is that which describes two types of love:

> "I have loved thee with two loves, a selfish love and a love that is worthy,
>> As for the love which is selfish, I occupy myself therein with remembrance of thee to the exclusion of all others,
>> As for that which is worthy of thee, therein thou raisest the veil that I may see thee."[1]

Like Christian nuns Rabia renounced marriage and remained celibate all her long life, preferring to espouse a heavenly Bridegroom, of whom she spoke so often in love: "My Beloved is with me alway, and for his love I can find no substitute." This language is very close to Christian mysticism and Hindu Bhakti.

Attar of Nishapur (died 1230) was biographer of Rabia, and himself a mystic. He wrote:

> "In Love no longer 'thou' and 'I' exist,
> For Self has passed away in the Beloved . . .
> He who would know the secret of both worlds,
> Will find the secret of them both is Love."[2]

Love to God and union with him, almost identification with him, was the message of Hallaj, who was martyred in Baghdad in A.D. 922.

[1] M. Smith, *Rabia the Mystic*, pp. 28, 30, 102.
[2] M. Smith, *The Persian Mystics, Attar*, p. 93.

"I am he whom I love, and he whom I love is I,
We are two spirits dwelling in one body,
If thou seest me, thou seest him,
And if thou seest him, thou seest us both."

It will be realized that such teaching would shock the orthodox who believed in a distant monarch God, especially as Hallaj set up the authority of his own personal experience against the authority of the Muslim church and state. But Hallaj lived and died for his faith, and as he was led out to be crucified he prayed for his executioners: "Forgive them, O Lord, and have mercy upon them; for verily if thou hadst revealed to them that which thou hast revealed to me, they would not have done what they have done."[1]

Other mystics, such as Ansari of Herat (died 1090), also stressed the importance of inward religion rather than outward:

"Know that the Prophet built an external Kaba
Of clay and water,
And an inner Kaba in life and heart.
The outer Kaba was built by Abraham,
The Holy;
The inner is sanctified by the glory of
God Himself."[2]

Among many mystical writers mention must be made of Al-Ghazali (died A.D. 1111), the great Persian philosopher, called "the proof of Islam", who did much to gain recognition for Sufi ideals in Islam.

Finally, the greatest mystical poet of Persia was Rumi (died 1273). His Mathnawi, "spiritual couplets", has been called "the Quran of Persia". Rumi develops the teaching of the unity of the worshipper with God, which other Sufis had stressed:

"O thou whose soul is free from 'we' and 'I' . . .
Thou didst contrive this 'I' and 'we' in order to play
the game of worship with thyself,

[1] R. A. Nicholson in *The Legacy of Islam*, pp. 217–18.
[2] S. J. Singh, *The Persian Mystics, Ansari*, p. 35.

That all 'I's' and 'thou's' might become one soul and
    at last be submerged in the Beloved."

Like some others Rumi saw in the differing sects and religions
separate ways to one goal:

"The lamps are different, but the Light is the same: it
    comes from Beyond.
O thou who art the kernel of existence, the disagreement
    between Muslim, Zoroastrian and Jew depends on
    the standpoint."

Love alone, said Rumi, can heal religious divisions, for "the
lovers of God have no religion but God alone".

"These two-and-seventy sects will remain till the Resur-
    rection . . .
Love alone can end their quarrel, Love alone comes to the
    rescue when you cry for help against their arguments,
Eloquence is dumbfounded by Love."[1]

ISLAM TO-DAY

Islam is a living religion and as such liable to change.
Although two centuries ago Islam might have appeared to be
petrified, and destined to be swept away by the impact of the
western world, yet there has been revival as well as adjustment
to new conditions. It is exceedingly difficult to estimate this,
since the Muslim world stretches from Africa to China and
varies greatly in different places, but some remarks may be
made.

Throughout the nineteenth century the forces of European
life broke into the Muslim world, on the one hand causing
liberal movements of reform to appear, and on the other
hand giving rise to puritanical reactions against the West,
such as the Wahhabi movement. But even in Wahhabi
Arabia motor-cars jostle camels, and whisky is consumed
before the eyes of the faithful.

European laws and codes came to be imposed in Egypt,
India, and elsewhere, leaving the traditional Quranic laws to

[1] R. A. Nicholson, *Rumi, Poet and Mystic*, pp. 33, 166, 173.

be applied in personal and family matters. European rule, however long it has lasted, in North Africa, the Middle East, and India, has left a deep impress upon Muslim life and thought.

Revolutionary changes have taken place in many Muslim lands. The abolition of the Caliphate by the Turks in 1924 was a shock to the whole Islamic world. Although for centuries the Caliphate had only been a name, yet it had a sentimental value. Recently the question of its restoration has been raised again in Pakistan.

More important than political and material changes is the question of the adaptation of Islamic teaching to the thought of the modern world. Modern science, historical criticism, and philosophy pose questions which demand an answer. Christianity has been shaken by such questions, and has had to submit her sacred documents to searching examination. Will Islam do the same? If not, will it hold its own in face of the education of youth by western methods in Muslim lands? It is in Pakistan that some of the boldest efforts have been made to combine the best in western thought with Muslim teaching. The university of Aligarh was founded with that express purpose.

The accretions of ages are being questioned. The supremacy of the Quran over its commentators is asserted, but there are Muslims who agree that Muhammad is its author. The ancient laws, particularly those commanding the subjection and seclusion of women, are radically changing in many lands. On the other hand, there are voices crying fiercely for a blind return to the past and a repudiation of the modern world and all its ways.

True religion goes deeper than either tradition or criticism. To the non-Muslim it is the Sufi who speaks the most abiding language and who stretches out his hand to others of like mind. But many Muslims know little of the mystics. To them the faith and brotherhood of Islam are of greatest importance.

Short Bibliography, of cheap modern books

A. Guillaume, *Islam* (Pelican Books)

H. A. R. Gibb, *Mohammedanism* (Home University Library)

A. S. Tritton, *Islam* (Hutchinson's University Library)

B. Lewis, *The Arabs in History* (Hutchinson)

J. M. Rodwell, *The Koran* (Everyman's Library)

E. H. Palmer, *The Koran* (World's Classics)

R. A. Nicholson, *Rumi* (Allen & Unwin)

M. Smith, *Readings from the Mystics of Islam* (Luzac)

E. Dermenghem, *Muhammad* (Longmans)

3

Indian Religion

THE BEGINNINGS

OF all the religions in the world those of India are the most complex, the most fascinating, and the most difficult to describe. Sir Charles Eliot in his great tomes on Indian religion says, "Any attempt to describe Hinduism as one whole leads to startling contrasts. The same religion enjoins self-mortification and orgies: commands human sacrifices and yet counts it a sin to eat meat or crush an insect: has more priests, rites, and images than ancient Egypt or medieval Rome and yet outdoes Quakers in rejecting all externals."

Eliot develops this theme by explaining: "Hinduism has not been made but has grown. It is a jungle, not a building. It is a living example of a great national paganism such as might have existed in Europe if Christianity had not become the state religion of the Roman Empire, if there had remained an incongruous jumble of old local superstititions, Greek philosophy, and oriental cults." Yet despite all this there is a bond of union within the religion because the different religious beliefs "became Indian and smack of the soil".[1]

The religion of most Indians to-day is generally called Hinduism. Both the words Hindu and India are derived from the Sanskrit (the ancient Indian liturgical language) meaning "river", a word applied especially to the Indus river in north-western India, the region best known to the Persians and Greeks of ancient times. But within the general term Hinduism we shall have to distinguish Brahmanism as an ancient and priestly form of religion.

[1] *Hinduism and Buddhism*, Vol. I, pp. xvii, 41.

A vast population, estimated at about 300 millions, is now described as Hindu. In the Indian sub-continent (including Pakistan) there are also about ninety million Muslims. There are important minority sects, such as Jains and Sikhs, to which reference will be made later. The great religion of Buddhism also arose in India and cannot be understood without the background of Indian thought, although Buddhism has now spread elsewhere and has almost entirely disappeared in the land of its origin.

A large and diverse "scripture", oral and written, is found all down Indian history from about 1000 B.C. onwards. The oldest religious books, the Vedas, are not, as is sometimes said, the most ancient religious documents in the world, although they contain traditions that were passed on orally for centuries before being written down. Of this and later literature short specimens will be given in due course.

About two centuries ago, European scholars studying the Sanskrit language noticed the remarkable resemblances that exist between Sanskrit and Latin and Greek. They agreed that these languages must have had a common origin, and that the peoples who spoke the original tongues had been dispersed eastwards to India and westwards to Europe. Before long the name Indo-European was coined to express the related tongues and peoples.

The Indo-Europeans are believed to have come from regions somewhere near the Caspian Sea. About 2000 B.C. there seem to have been related tribes from South Russia to Turkestan who had similar culture and spoke dialects of the Indo-European type. They began to disperse about the beginning of the sixteenth century B.C., and invaded Mesopotamia, for example. In the remains of the ancient Hittite kingdom in Asia Minor there have recently been discovered clay tablets which refer to the gods Mitra, Varuna, and Indra who feature in the later Vedas in India.

Somewhere between 1500 and 1200 B.C. (the period when the Israelites were coming out of Egypt) Indo-European invaders poured into India, settling first of all in the Punjab in the north and later moving on eastward. In the Vedas these peoples call themselves Aryan, "noble" or "lord" (Sanskrit *arya*, Persian *ariya*). They fought with the dark-skinned and flat-nosed natives of the country, and called them Dasas, squat creatures, a word which came to mean slave.

The castes into which Hindu society came to be divided were partly based on this racial distinction of light from dark skins. The Indian word for the four main castes is *varna*, which means colour. The castes were thus social rather than religious. But to-day, after all these centuries, the colour of the skin is no indication of caste.

It used to be thought that the Aryan invaders met only savages who contributed nothing to later Indian religion. There seemed no evidence of earlier religion. Even Eliot in 1921 wrote that ancient India has yielded "no religious antiquities, nor is it probable that such will be discovered". But in the last forty years intensive excavations have been made at several places in the Indus area. Particularly at Harappa and Mohenjodaro ("the place of the dead") have remains of large cities been discovered which represent a complex urban civilization.

The Aryans were still mainly a pastoral people, and they descended on the ancient Indus civilization of the Dasas with their horse-drawn chariots, ascribing their conquests to their gods, particularly Indra the destroyer of forts. In the Vedas we read:

> "With all-outstripping chariot wheel, O Indra,
>   Thou far-famed, hast overthrown twice ten
>   kings of men."

The Vedas only give us the Aryan point of view. There is scorn of the physique and the barbaric speech of the Dasas, and they are called "indifferent to the gods". But this is not true. Excavations have shown that the Dasas had their own gods, and it is probable that more of their religion was taken up into later Hinduism than used to be admitted likely.

Among the many objects unearthed at Harappa and Mohenjodaro are large numbers of human statuettes, most of which are female. They seem to indicate cults of a mother-goddess, giver of life and fertility, such as were known in other

33

lands, and as survived in Hinduism in Śaktism, the worship of the female principle in nature. An important seal of about 2000 B.C. has been found at Mohenjodaro, of a three-faced figure, with a headdress of horns, sitting down and accompanied by animals. It resembles Śiva, one of the greatest gods of later Hinduism, who is often represented with several faces, and sits as a yogi ascetic. Śiva is called the lord of beasts.[1]

Sir John Marshall, writing of Mohenjodaro and the ancient Indus civilization, says, "Their religion is so characteristically Indian as hardly to be distinguishable from still living Hinduism or at least from that aspect of it which is bound up with animism and the cults of Śiva and the Mother Goddess—still the two most potent forces in popular worship."[2]

It must be affirmed, however, that the religion of the Vedic books seems to owe little to the Indus civilization. Until the inscriptions at Harappa have been deciphered we cannot say how much effect one religion had on the other. It is in later Hinduism, after Vedic times, that we find forms of religions that probably existed much earlier.

VEDISM OR BRAHMANISM

A. *The Vedas*

The above introduction was necessary to give us the setting for the first literary records in the Vedas. The religion of these books is sometimes called Vedism, or Brahmanism, as it was developed by the Brahmin priests. Vedism was in the hands of a priestly class who served a military aristocracy. The masses of the people may already have followed a religion like that of later Hinduism.

The word *veda* is a Sanskrit noun which means knowledge. It denotes knowledge or wisdom that is passed down in the collection of sacred books. There are four main books, the Rig-Veda, Sama-Veda, Yajur-Veda, and Atharva-Veda. The last three contain liturgies, prayers, and formulas for incantation.

[1] The palatal sibilant (soft sh) is written ś, as in Śiva. The cerebral sibilant ṣ is written sh, as in Vishnu.

[2] *Mohenjo-daro and the Indus Civilization*, Vol. I, p. vii.

The oldest and most important is the Rig-Veda or Song Veda. It comprises 1,028 hymns to the gods arranged in ten sub-divisions or circles. The Rig-Veda may have been completed by 800 B.C. It has close resemblances to the sacred Gatha books of Zoroastrianism in Persia which are somewhat later.

The Vedas are sophisticated priestly writings, and they are not so simple as they appear at first sight. The gods (*deva*, cf. Latin *deus*) of the Vedas number thirty-three, divided between the regions of sky, air, and earth. They are nature-gods, but are spoken of as human. There seems to be no Supreme Being over all. True there is Dyaus Pitar, the bright sky, whose name is the same as the Greek Zeus and the Latin Jupiter. But he is far away and has practically no myths told about him. He has Prthivi, Mother Earth, as consort.

One of the most prominent gods is Varuna (possibly the Greek Ouranos, heaven) who, while without myth, upholds the moral and physical law. He is addressed in the most exalted prayers:

> "Varuna, true to holy law, sits down among his
>   people; he,
> Most wise, sits there to govern all.
> From thence perceiving, he beholds all wondrous
>   things, both what hath been,
> And what hereafter will be done."[1]

A rather shadowy companion of Varuna is Mitra, the same as the Persian Mithra whose cult spread all over Europe in the Roman era.

Varuna became for a time pre-eminent in Vedic religion, almost the supreme God. But instead of developing as such a leading god did in Persia and Greece, Varuna gradually faded out. There is not a single temple to him in India to-day.

We have met Indra, god of the storm and great warrior-god of the invading Aryans. He is the most prominent god in the Rig-Veda, one quarter of the hymns being dedicated to him. He is followed by a troop of lesser storm gods. Indra is a

[1] N. Macnicol, *Hindu Scriptures*, pp. 4, 5.

non-moral nature god, a great drinker of the sacred drink (*soma*).

> "I will declare the manly deeds of Indra, the first that he
> achieved, the thunder-wielder.
> He slew the dragon, then disclosed the waters, and cleft
> the channels of the mountain torrents . . .
> Impetuous as a bull, he chose the soma, and in three
> sacred beakers drank the juices."[1]

The power of the sacred alcohol (*soma*) is ascribed to divine agency, and the drink gradually becomes personified as a god. A power like the Soma is Agni, the god of fire (Old Latin *ignis*). Agni is a natural force bringing light and warmth to men, but terrible in destruction: "Fire-jawed, wind-driven, there blazes down upon the wood Agni, like a strong bull that rushes on the herd."

There is also Rudra, another dangerous god, originally a storm god, and symbolized by a bull. He is perhaps the prototype of the later great god Śiva. Only a few hymns of the Rig-Veda are devoted to Vishnu, the god who, like Śiva, becomes of first importance in medieval and modern Hinduism.

The mythology of the Vedas is not too clear. But efforts have been made to trace out the principal themes. There is a creation myth which begins with the cosmic waters and a great Fashioner, Tvastri, who made the divine pair, sky and earth. They were parents of the gods who quarrelled among themselves until Indra, fortified with Soma, won the battle and finally Varuna gave the laws.

The famous Creation Hymn towards the end of the Rig-Veda is much more sophisticated than the earlier hymns. It arises in a stage of transition when the very gods are being questioned and are regarded as themselves the products of some mysterious being:

> "Who verily knows and who can here declare it, whence
> it was born and whence comes this creation?
> The gods are later than this world's production. Who
> knows, then, whence it first came into being?

[1] N. Macnicol, *Hindu Scriptures*, p. 6.

He, the first origin of this creation, whether he formed it
  all or did not form it,
Whose eye controls this world in highest heaven, he
  verily knows it, or perhaps he knows it not."[1]

Most of the gods of the Vedas disappear in later times, and
its apparently carefree polytheism gives way to asceticism and
pessimism. The seeds of some of the later priestly beliefs and
claims are in the Vedas: "We drank Soma, we became
immortal, we found the gods."

But it must not be thought that a study of the Vedas is
merely of historical interest. The authority of the Vedas was
constantly reaffirmed in later ages. Moreover, some of the
reform movements of the last century, notably the Arya-
Samaj, have returned to the Vedas for inspiration.

Some of the Vedic prayers are still used daily in India.
Every morning devout Hindus repeat this verse of the Rig-
Veda in their prayers and as grace at meals: "Let us meditate
on the most excellent light of the Creator, may he guide our
intellects." This is the sacred sentence (*mantra*), called the
gayatri, as popular in India as the Lord's Prayer is to Christians,
and which every Brahmin and every householder is expected
to recite over two million times during his life.

B. *The Upanishads*

In time each of the four Vedas had a body of commentaries
attached to it, which contained directions for the performance
of the sacrificial ritual. These commentaries are called
Brahmanas, and they are long dull formulas by the use of
which the priests conducted their exceedingly complex rites.

The word Brahma seems originally in Sanskrit to have
meant "magical spell" and later "sacred rite". The priests
were called Brahmans, usually spelt Brahmin in English which
is incorrect but useful because it helps to distinguish the priest
from the further use of the word Brahman to denote the
Supreme Being.

The Brahmins regarded themselves as supermen, human
gods, because by performing their rites they made the very

[1] Op. cit., p. 37.

37

sun to rise. They claimed the monopoly of religion, excluding some castes from its observance. To-day the Brahmin caste has been called "a hereditary guild possessing secret professional knowledge". They still claim superior birth to other men. But not all Brahmins are now priests; the majority follow other vocations. And, on the other hand, many priests of Indian temples are not Brahmins, the temple worship being different from the elaborate ceremonial with which the Brahmin should be occupied.

Attached to and later than the Brahmanas are the famous Upanishads. The Sanskrit word Upanishad seems originally to have meant "session", used of pupils sitting round a teacher, and thence developing into "communication" and "secret teaching". This is appropriate for the dialogue form in which these writings are often cast. The Upanishads later came to be called Vedanta, the "end" of the Vedas. Long after writing had come into use, the Vedas, Brahmanas, and Upanishads were only handed down orally. As sacred matters they must not be published or uttered before members of lower castes. By great feats of memory they were retained until they were eventually written, some time in the Christian era.

Whereas the Vedas are chiefly hymns, and the Brahmanas are concerned with ritual, the Upanishads are theological and philosophical treatises. They present the philosophical development of Indian thought. After a time of decay, and the formalism of the Brahmanas, there seems to come a spiritual revival in which some of the most penetrating questions concerning men and the world are put and answered in a way that became typical of India.

The age of the Upanishads is uncertain, but probably most of them date from some time after 800 B.C. There have been more than three hundred Upanishads, but the most important of the really old ones that survive number thirteen. The Upanishads teach the importance of repetition and meditation as a means of concentrating thought. "Let a man meditate on the syllable Om." Om was a sacred syllable that had to be pronounced at the repetition of every Veda. By reiterating it one should realize the cause of the universe.

In the Upanishads the robust Vedic gods have gone. Indra is presented as a Brahmin student. The cause and ground of all existence is now stated to be Brahman. This word becomes "the sacred", the soul of the universe, the Supreme Being. One Upanishad begins with the question:

"The Brahma-students say: Is Brahman the cause? Whence are we born? Whereby do we live, and whither do we go?"

And the answer comes:

"The Highest Brahman is the safe support, the imperishable. The Brahma-students, when they have known what is within this world, are devoted and merged in the Brahman, free from birth."[1]

The name of the soul or spirit of man was Atman. The Upanishads direct their thoughts towards showing that Brahman and Atman are identical. This is the principle of "non-duality" (advaita). Brahman is the great Self of the universe, the one Atman. Not only so, but since Brahman is in man, man is in Brahman, and indeed is Brahman.

"He from whom all works, all desires, all sweet odours and tastes proceed, who embraces all this, who never speaks and is never surprised, he, my self within the heart, is that Brahman."

In a famous dialogue in the Chandogya Upanishad a father is talking with his son, Svetaketu. He tells him to put some salt in water, and when it is found that the salt disappears but is tasted in every part of the water, that shows that the universal self is diffused throughout the universe and yet is present in the individual.

"That which is the subtle essence, in it all that exists has its self. It is the True. It is the Self, and thou, O Svetaketu, art it."[2]

This last phrase runs through the Upanishads, "That thou art" (tat twam asi). So we have the teaching that the Self is

[1] Op. cit., pp. 210–11.   [2] Ibid., pp. 142, 173.

39

Brahman and Brahman is the sole reality. This is believed to bring peace and deliverance from the world and from rebirth.

Such a radical doctrine goes far beyond the gods of the Vedas. Gods and men are all part of the universal Self. So the polytheism of the early days is changed into a monism (only one existent) in which there is only one Self. The gods are merged into this universal Self. Another dialogue asks, "How many gods are there really?" It receives the answer, "One." And that One is incomprehensible and can only be described by negatives: "That Self is to be described by 'No, no!' He is incomprehensible, for he cannot be comprehended; he is imperishable, for he cannot perish."

This brings also a reaction against sacrifices, for one is saved by knowledge and union with the one self. "And when they say, 'Sacrifice to this or sacrifice to that god', each god is but his manifestation, for he is all gods."

A further doctrine of the Upanishads is the reincarnation of souls. This doctrine of rebirth is strange to modern Europe, but it was taught by Plato and is well known in Africa. But it also has difficulty in fitting into Brahmanic ideas, for they taught, as we have seen, a salvation by merging into identity with the universal soul. Rebirth introduces moral ideas; by good action one gets free from this world and its trials.

The Sanskrit word *samsara* is used to express the idea of "migration", the rebirth of the soul in an endless series of bodies. One's lot in the next life is determined by the consequences of deeds done in this life, by one's *karma* (deed). This became particularly a Buddhist doctrine, but it is also taught in the Upanishads that those who do good in this life will obtain a better birth and those who do wickedly get a worse birth.

"Those whose conduct has been good, will quickly attain some good birth, the birth of a Brahmana, or a Kshatriya, or a Vaiśya. But those whose conduct has been evil, will quickly attain an evil birth, the birth of a dog, or a hog, or a Chandala" (outcaste).[1]

[1] Op. cit., p. 161.

Many races have believed in rebirth, but in India the belief has been qualified by the thought of its undesirability. Connected with it is the notion that the whole visible world is evil or an illusion (*maya; mayin* means magician). Life is evil, and to be bound to this world in an endless chain of rebirths is a fearful destiny. Therefore deliverance must be sought, and it can be won by the knowledge of the truth of the unity of the soul and Brahman, and through ascetic discipline and moral effort. That frees man from the round of existence.

The ties that bind man to life and to rebirth are his desires. If these can be completely eliminated, then he may be no more reborn, but may sink himself into the universal Self:

"When all desires which once entered his heart are undone, then does the mortal become immortal, then he obtains Brahman. . . . As the flowing rivers disappear in the sea, losing their name and their form, thus a wise man, freed from name and form, goes to the divine Person, who is greater than the great."

THE RISE OF JAINISM AND BUDDHISM

In this period of philosophical development, the sixth century B.C., there arose two movements in North India which are closely connected with the speculations and disciplines of the time, but eventually become religious and philosophical systems in their own right. Jainism has remained quite small in numbers, with only something over one million adherents to-day. Buddhism has become a great world missionary religion, but almost entirely outside India.

It is interesting to note that the founders of both these religions were members of the warrior caste, the Kshatriyas, and not Brahmins. They lived in the same century. There has been some debate as to which religion is the elder, but it seems probable that it is Jainism.

The Jains claim that their religion was founded by twenty-four great ascetics, of which the historical founder was only the last. These founders are called Jinas, conquerors or "forders", and hence their followers are called Jainas or Jains.

41

Mahavira (Great Hero), as the last of the Jinas is called, was named Vardhamana, and born about 599 B.C. He married and had a child, but he renounced his wife and child when his parents undertook a fast unto death, which later became a practice of some Jains. Then Mahavira gave up worldly life and the wearing of clothes, and became a wandering ascetic practising austerities and suffering persecution. After fourteen years he felt that he had solved the riddle of existence and gained enlightenment. For the following thirty years, until his death in 527, he lived a wandering life preaching his doctrine at the head of a group of devotees.

Jainism takes over the current Indian ideas of the soul, rebirth, and *karma* (action, deeds). But it denies the existence of a Supreme Being (though not of other gods), and it considers that there are many individual souls which exist from all eternity. In direct opposition to Buddhism it teaches the existence of the Self as a stable and eternal principle.

Jainism regards *karma* as a poison of the soul, and it teaches ascetic methods to destroy old *karma* and ward off new. It abandons the Brahmin idea that salvation comes through knowledge, and replaces this by good conduct. So it teaches purity and morality.

Jainism extends its moral teaching not only to all human beings but to all life. It puts forth the doctrine of "harmlessness" (*ahimsa*), by which one must not harm or kill any living creature. Although in origin this doctrine seems to have arisen from the desire to keep oneself unspotted from the world, yet as it developed it became a practice of compassion. "One may not kill, nor ill use, nor insult, nor torment, nor persecute any kind of living being, any kind of creature, any kind of thing having a soul, any kind of beings. That is the pure, eternal, enduring commandment of religion which has been proclaimed by the sages who comprehend the world."

This teaching of *ahimsa* is one of the most attractive features of Jainism, and has led to kindly and gentle conduct. The Jains forbid animal sacrifices, the eating of meat, and hunting. They strain their drink, and screen lamps to avoid harming insects. They tend sick animals.

The aim of life is oneself to become a Jina or conqueror. To this end groups of monks were formed to renounce the world and engage in self-denying discipline. The earlier Jinas receive great veneration and, strangely enough, this atheistic system has its temples containing images of the Jinas to which the laity bring their offerings.

The Jain scriptures, Purvas and Angas and non-canonical literature, are long and tedious. They seem somewhat older than the scriptures of Buddhism, but the two movements ran side by side for long and have some common features.

"Where do the perfected souls reside? Where do they leave their bodies, and where do they go on reaching perfection?

Perfected souls reside on the top of the world; they leave their bodies here, and go there, on reaching perfection."[1]

Jainism was not a missionary religion, as Buddhism was later, and did little to spread its doctrines. To-day some Jain groups are publishing literature outside their own territory, and their great principle of non-violence or harmlessness has attracted the attention of many people outside their own ranks. Mahatma Gandhi adopted this principle in his life and work.

Only passing reference will be made to Buddhism here, since such a great and extensive religion demands treatment on its own. It is simply necessary to call attention to the fact that Buddhism arose in the same century as Jainism, and against the background of similar thought.

Gotama the Buddha helped to undermine the caste system and the proud attitude of the Brahmins. This had two effects. It aroused the animosity of the Brahmins, and contributed to the eventual disappearance of Buddhism from India. But it also helped Buddhism to spread outside India. In a sense, Buddhism is Indian influence exported elsewhere. Hinduism is a national religion. To be a Hindu it is not sufficient to believe in the sacred scriptures, one must belong to a Hindu caste and keep its regulations. Buddhism cuts free from this,

[1] *Sacred Books of the East*, XLV, p. 211.

and takes Indian ideas to other lands, incorporating other elements on its way.

Buddhism has also been called atheistic, although this has been debated. It was more correctly agnostic. Certainly later Buddhism has its many saints and gods. The Buddha is said to have asked how the invisible Brahman could be an object of worship. But Brahman was little worshipped, anyway, in Vedism or later Hinduism. Buddhism attacked sacrifices, but on the whole the main body of belief was accepted. Buddhism teaches rebirth, *karma*, and *nirvana* (going out). It differs from the Upanishads and Jainism in its denial of the existence of the self, and the substitution for this of a series of states of consciousness.

It has often been asked why, since the Buddha was an Indian, Buddhism has virtually disappeared from India. The opposition of the Brahmins has been noted. It seems probable that Buddhism was not such a popular movement in India as it became elsewhere; in its early forms it was perhaps too austere for the masses. It was largely confined to monasteries and schools, being monastic like Jainism. Buddhism enjoyed royal patronage in several periods. The great king Aśoka (died 232 B.C.) did a great deal to spread Buddhism. Later a schism appeared which permanently divided Buddhism into two main camps. Later still the Gupta empire, from A.D. 320, did much to support Hindu orthodoxy. There were also the strong popular Hindu beliefs in a personal deity that were against Buddhist teaching. Finally the Muslim conquest, from A.D. 700 to 1200, brought persecution and destruction to many Buddhist monasteries.

Buddhism left its mark on India. The Brahmins and the sacrificial system never recovered their ancient power. While India rejected the Buddha's monastic way, yet it was deeply affected by his moral teaching by which men obtain deliverance from rebirth. To-day there is a revival of interest in the Buddha as the greatest of the sons of India.

Yet the masses of the Indian people remained Hindu. Some scholars speak of a renaissance of Hinduism towards the end of the Buddhist period. Others maintain that Hinduism had not diminished in strength. It is just that our records are faulty, and no doubt there was plenty of vigorous Hindu life all down the two millenniums of our era.

LATER HINDUISM: A RELIGION OF INCARNATIONS

The Upanishads gave philosophical teaching for thinkers and ascetics. Their impersonal teaching of the Deity prepared the way for the virtual atheism of Jain and Buddhist doctrine. But had ancient India no more profoundly religious and popular teaching than this? Indeed it had.

Indian religious history has sometimes been divided into an older period of Brahmanism, and a later period of Hinduism proper with its many sects. In another way, the division has been made between Aryan and non-Aryan (Dasa or Dravidian). But these divisions assume both that Hinduism itself is not very old, and also that Vedism did not influence the later religion. This is not so. Hinduism is the expression of an ancient and living great civilization, and the famous Bhagavadgita develops Brahmin thought.

What is evident in later Hinduism is an opposite movement from the impersonal teaching of the Upanishads, and a stress on belief in a personal God. There are already traces of this in the later Upanishads, with a personal Lord (*Iśvara*) replacing the impersonal Brahman.

The religion of personal devotion centres round the gods Vishnu and Śiva. Vishnu had appeared as a minor character in the Vedas, but now he emerges as supreme and as appearing on earth in successive incarnations. Although a Vedic god, it is considered possible that Vishnu became pre-eminent in Hinduism because of links with pre-Aryan religion, and possibly also due to the stimulus of new ideas from outside India.

This theistic Hinduism is expressed first in two great epic poems, the Ramayana and the Mahabharata. They were probably completed by the second century A.D., but it is considered that their origin goes back to the pre-Buddhist period.

The Ramayana, Career of Rama, is a very long work of over 24,000 couplets. It was written in Sanskrit by Valmiki, but there are other popular versions at later dates, notably that by the mystic Tulsidas. It has been translated into most Indian languages and is still widely used. By its story of marital devotion it exerts a healthy influence on family life.

The Ramayana is a tale of northern India where lived an ideal king Rama and his wife Sita. It tells of their adventures; how Sita was carried off by a demon Ravana, helped by Hanuman the monkey god, and finally rescued by Rama. This simple story gradually comes in later editions to be an account of the descent (*avatar*) of the god Vishnu in the form of Rama to slay the demon Ravana. The incarnation of Vishnu in Rama is said to have been the seventh descent of the god, Krishna is the eighth *avatar*, and Buddha the ninth. The tenth *avatar* is yet to come; he is Kalki, a sort of Messiah.

Thus we have the belief expressed in recurrent incarnations or descents of Vishnu, but as unreal or visionary appearances, rather than like the Christian teaching of the Word once made "flesh" in history. There is also the deification of Rama and Krishna, in so far as they were historical or traditional human figures. Rama and Krishna, indeed, as personal gods over-shadow Vishnu, especially in northern India.

The Mahabharata is much longer than the Ramayana, and has 90,000 couplets. The title means the "great Bharata" story, and it tells of the war of the house of Bharata and a neighbouring north Indian tribe. It resembles the Iliad in its stories of divine chiefs, especially of two of them, Arjuna and Karna.

The most important part of the Mahabharata is an inserted section in the sixth book. This is the Bhagavad-Gita, the Song of the Lord, or Song of the Blessed One. The Gita (as this title is abridged) has often been called the most important single work ever produced in India, the "New Testament of India," the "Gospel of Krishna". It is read and loved as no other book in India to-day. It is also misunderstood and idealized. There are many translations in English. It is a short poem, about as long as St John's Gospel. Its date is debated, but it was probably written somewhere about the beginning of the Christian era.

The Gita is in the form of a dialogue between the warrior

Arjuna and Krishna who is his charioteer, and who is gradually revealed in his true godlike nature to Arjuna. Arjuna is paralysed by indecision before the battle, and asks himself whether it is right to kill his kinsfolk. To this important question Krishna replies, first that Arjuna must do his duty as a member of the warrior caste, and further that killing is unreal since the soul never dies. Slayer and slain are Brahman who himself is never slain.

"The unborn, the permanent, the eternal, the ancient, it is not slain when the body is slain. . . . Therefore for no creature shouldst thou sorrow."

This teaching is of course Brahmanic. Action is dictated by caste obligations. If a man kills it has been determined by God. In any case the soul is deathless. The world itself is only a play (*maya*) which God acts with himself. Yet with this harsh teaching there are also mingled other elements that have endeared the Gita to millions.

Krishna teaches Arjuna that not only fighting but all actions should be undertaken without thought of reward. To free oneself from desire, and from the fruit of actions (*karma*), the method of Yoga is taught. Yoga, mental training (from the same root as the English word yoke), appears as a technique of meditation. This was not new, but it is made available in the Gita for everyone.

"A Yogi should constantly train his self, staying in a secret place, alone, controlling his mind, free from hope and possessions.

In a pure place, setting up for himself a firm seat, not too high, not too low, with cloth, antelope skin, and kusa grass upon it,

There bringing his mind to one point, restraining the action of the mind and senses, and sitting on the seat, he should practise Yoga for the purifying of the self."[1]

The Gita combines both the Brahmanic non-ethical teaching, and a moral teaching of kindness and compassion.

[1] E. J. Thomas, *The Song of the Lord*, pp. 58–9.

"He who is without hatred to any being, who is friendly and compassionate, not thinking of mine or myself, balanced in pleasure and pain, patient,

Who is ever content, practising Yoga, with his self restrained, his conviction firm, his mind and intellect dedicated to me, devoted to me, that man is dear to me."[1]

The moral teaching is that of indifference, of restrained self-seeking to avoid defilement. No doubt in practice feelings of compassion have often dominated the actions of the Yogi. The last phrase of this quotation brings out a further great teaching of the Gita, "devotion to me". Devotion to Krishna the god is made the motive of action. Love to God is an end in itself. So the Gita ends:

"Have thy mind on me, be devoted to me, sacrifice to me, do reverence to me. To me shalt thou come; what is true I promise; dear art thou to me.

Abandoning all duties come to me, the one refuge; I will free thee from all sins; sorrow not."

This shows that the song is not just an incident in a battle, but is an allegory with a mystical interpretation. It must be noted, however, that there is no question of a God of love, but One who is above good and evil, with whom the Yogi seeks identification.

It is thought that the Gita was originally a verse Upanishad, which was later modified to become the charter of the personal religion of Krishna. This picture of devotion to God has taken great hold on many Hindu minds, as a relief from philosophical theology. Its teaching of the unselfish performance of duty and personal devotion to Krishna, which can be practised in everyday life, has won for the Gita a secure place in the affections of modern Hindus.

THE DEVELOPMENT OF BHAKTI

The loving devotion to a personal God is called *Bhakti*, and this has been a persistent feature of Hinduism during most of

[1] Ibid., pp. 92, 121–2.

the last two millenniums. It is especially connected with the worship of Vishnu and his *avatars* and with Śiva.

One of the principal gods who is worshipped with Bhakti is Krishna (often called Hari), the most popular of the *avatars* of Vishnu. In addition to what has been said of him in the Gita, Krishna has other features. Some think he was originally a historical figure, but he has many mythical stories told of him. The name Krishna means black, it is mentioned in the Upanishads and in Buddhist writings, but it is in the Mahabharata and later "ancient tales" (Puranas) that he figures principally. Many legends are told of his youth. He was brought up by a herdsman and spent his time sporting with the milkmaids of whom he is said to have married over a thousand. These and other fantastic and licentious stories come from folk-tales, and possibly from the myths of earlier nature gods like the Greek Dionysus. Krishna is associated with all kinds of love, from amorous sport to the mystical love of God. Although some of the rites commemorating Krishna's loves have brought discredit on his cult, it must be said that the best mystical writers interpret these stories as dealing with the most chaste love.

Śiva is a more difficult god for a non-Hindu to understand, although he is very popular. For instead of the benevolence of Vishnu we have terror and sexuality. Śiva is generally taken to be a development from Rudra (red), a storm-god of the Vedas. He may well be a very ancient pre-Aryan deity. As storm-god and sender of disease, he can withhold these plagues and grant health, thus becoming kindly. Wherefore he is prayed, "Slay us not, for thou art gracious."

A well-known image depicts Śiva, with four arms, dancing as the Life-force. Perhaps he is best understood thus, as the terrible wielder of the forces of life and death, and the giver of sexual fertility. His most common emblem is a stone pillar, the *lingam*, a sexual symbol though usually of decent appearance.

Śiva has no *avatars* or incarnations, but goddesses are associated with him, especially Kali, the Great Goddess (*Mahadevi*), an ogress who demands bloody sacrifices. Kali is

49

much feared, and ugly and obscene rites have been connected with her cult. Yet it must be said that not only are these rites changing, but also that symbols which may have been sexual in origin no longer have such meanings to many worshippers.

In South India Śiva is very popular and has beautiful temples dedicated to him. There are lovely hymns in the Tamil language which call Śiva the compassionate and the supreme God. Thus Manikka Vachakar in the tenth century writes of the Father-Mother love of Śiva:

> "O Mother! O Father! O Unequalled Light!
> O sweet Nectar born of love . . .
> In this life I hold thee in firm grip!
> How then canst thou leave me?"[1]

There are many other devotional poets of the Bhakti movements over the centuries. Mention can only be made here of Tulsidas in the sixteenth century, who wrote a Hindi version of the Ramayana which has become the Bible of many people in northern India. Tulsidas seems to be one of the nearest of Hindu writers to the religions which believe in a personal and sole God. He declared, "the worship of the Impersonal laid no hold on my heart". To him Rama is supreme and full of compassion:

> "One God there is . . . He hath become incarnate, and hath wrought manifold works out of pure love for them that believe on him. He is All-Gracious and Full of Compassion towards them that are lowly of heart, and in his Mercy he putteth away his wrath towards them that love him, and whom he knoweth as his own."[2]

Like some of the Muslim Sufis, Tulsidas adores God:

> "Ashamed, I dare not raise my eyes to meet thy sweet familiar face; and yet without adoring thee I am not at peace."

The Bhakti movements won acceptance by the efforts of philosophical writers who gave them doctrinal foundations.

[1] A. J. Appasamy, *Temple Bells*, p. 59.
[2] A. C. Bouquet, *Sacred Books of the World*, p. 225.

Śankara did this for the Śiva faith in the eighth century, though he honoured Vishnu also. Śankara is often spoken of as the chief author of the Vedanta. He taught the doctrine of non-duality (*advaita*), and maintained that there is only one absolute reality, the Brahman.

In the eleventh century, Ramanuja left the worship of Śiva for that of Vishnu, and he strongly opposed the philosophy of Śankara. His teaching is much more theistic, and affirms the reality both of the world and of God. The world arises and passes away endlessly in eternal repetition, for it is the outcome of the play (*lila*) of God. Ramanuja stressed the affection between God and the soul in the true Bhakti manner.

The Bhakti movement expressed the feelings of the common people and led to the creation of fine vernacular devotional literature. Both ordinary men and scholars have acknowledged its appeal. Still to-day many of the leaders of Hindu thought, such as Gandhi and Tagore, have used the Bhakti hymns in their religious activities.

HINDUISM AND ISLAM

The Sikhs

It will be realized that Islam and Hinduism are very different. The one is a stern monotheism and the other teaches absorption in the impersonal Brahman or devotion to various gods. Yet Islam has also become one of the Indian religions. Over the centuries Islam and Hinduism have both opposed and influenced one another, and at the mystical level there has been mingling. Islam represents the main impact of the western monotheistic religions upon the East, but this has not been without its effect on Islam itself.

Within a hundred years of the death of Muhammad the Muslim armies had entered India, occupying Sind in A.D. 712. Invasion soon stopped, but missionaries and emissaries of Persian trade and culture affected Indian life. With that tolerance which has been both a strength and a weakness to India, mosques were allowed to be built.

With the coming of the Turks, Sind and the Punjab were again invaded and annexed in 1022. In 1190 another wave from

Afghanistan captured Delhi and assumed the rule of much of North India. In 1400 the Turco-Mongol Timour ravaged Delhi again with great ferocity. Many Hindus suffered in these constant raids, but even more significant was the final destruction of Buddhism in India. It had survived longer in the north than in the south, but we read of massacres of monks and destruction of monasteries in Bihar and Benares in 1190. The Muslims fought all idolaters, but Buddhists who were centred at the monasteries were the worst sufferers. Henceforth they are to be found almost entirely outside India, except for Nepal and a few other places.

In 1526 the Turco-Mongol Babar seized Delhi and founded the great Mughal empire which lasted until the British conquest in 1757. The Mughals built many splendid palaces and tombs, though some of them also demolished fine Hindu temples. Their most famous monument is no doubt the white marble Taj Mahal at Agra, the tomb built by the emperor Shah Jehan for his favourite wife.

In India and Pakistan to-day there are over 90 million Muslims, divided between the two states. It is important to note that most Muslims are Indians or Pakistanis, and not foreigners. Not only did the invaders merge themselves into Indian life, but there were many conversions to Islam. These conversions went largely by groups and occupations, such as weavers and butchers, and so were the more numerous.

In some places, Indian Muslims have adopted Hindu customs. Even the caste system is reflected in the high and low class Muslims. In certain places low caste converts are not admitted into mosques. Some Muslim villagers still worship the local gods or use a sacred fire ritual. The catholicity of Hinduism is copied in the innumerable Indian Muslim sects, and in the many saints worshipped. The Hindu holy mendicant finds his counterpart in the Muslim *faqir*.

When the British withdrew from India and the Muslim state of Pakistan was formed, many millions of Muslims were left in the Indian state. There is popular pressure for them to become Hindu, just as there are neglected Hindu temples in Pakistan. India has decided to be a secular state, whereas in

Pakistan Islam is the state religion, with freedom promised to other religions.

From the fifteenth century efforts were made by a number of thinkers to combine the best in Hinduism and Islam. The earliest sect was founded by Kabir (born about 1440). He was a disciple of Ramananda, who, although a worshipper of Rama, said that the universal God may be worshipped anywhere, and he admitted all castes to his sect.

Kabir was a Muslim weaver of Benares, and he lived and taught in northern India. He stood midway between Islam and Hinduism, but with a leaning towards Hinduism. Kabir's shrine at Maghor (United Provinces) is shared by Hindus and Muslims—a unique phenomenon.

Kabir condemned idolatry, caste, avatars, and circumcision. But he believed in the sanctity of all life, and in rebirth. He used any divine name for God:

"If God be within the mosque, then to whom does this
world belong?
If Ram be within the image which you find upon your
pilgrimage, then who is there to know what happens
without? . . .
Look within your heart, for there you will find both
Karim and Ram.
All men and women of the world are his living forms.
Kabir is the child of Allah and Ram."[1]

Kabir is fully in the Bhakti tradition, and his poems express his love and joy in the presence of God. "Few are the lovers who know the Beloved", he sings. Or again, "More than all else do I cherish at heart that love which makes me to live a limitless life in this world."

It is generally held, though some dispute this, that Kabir influenced the founder of the Sikh religion, Nanak. Contrary to Kabir, Nanak (1469–1538) was born a Hindu but moved over to the side of Islam. He had a vision of the court of God, in which he was instructed to tell other people of the divine name.

[1] R. Tagore, *Kabir's Poems*, p. 72.

Nanak did not intend at first to found a sect, but disciples were attracted by his teaching. The word Sikh means "disciple". He declared, "There is no Hindu and no Muslim." This bold utterance, and his songs, attracted considerable attention. He passed his life partly in teaching and partly in retirement.

As a poet Nanak does not equal Kabir, but as a social and religious reformer he did much to bring Hindus and Muslims together. He strongly opposed formalism in worship, and inculcated devotion to one God.

"Love the Lord, O my soul . . .
    A well without water, a cow without milk, a shrine in
        darkness,
    So art thou without him, O my soul."[1]

The worship in Sikh temples begins with the sentence reminiscent of Islam: "There is but one God, whose name is true, the Creator."

With the fourth leader (guru) of the Sikhs many wealthy people were induced to join the movement, and the famous Golden Temple was built in the tank of Amritsar. The Holy Book of the Sikhs (the Granth) was compiled from hymns by Nanak, Kabir, and others. To-day the Granth lying open on a reading desk is seen in every Sikh temple, like the Bible in churches.

Persecution under the Mughals caused the Sikhs to take up arms, and henceforth they have regarded themselves as a military brotherhood, one of the characteristics of Islam, usually distasteful to Hinduism. Distinctive features were adopted for Sikhs which have remained as their badge: the hair must not be cut, a steel comb and bangle must be worn, together with shorts and a sword.

The fortunes of the Sikhs have varied. At times they have seemed to be merging into Hinduism; at others there has been a revival of the Sikh faith. Under the British they were loyal and favoured, providing large numbers of men for the army as well as taking easily to new western trades. More than any

[1] *Temple Bells*, p. 28.

others they suffered from the partition of India, and many thousands of Muslims and Sikhs were massacred when the latter were driven out of Pakistan. They were said to number over five million, but in India there is a tendency for them to be absorbed into Hinduism. One of their latest writers says, "If the present pace of amalgamation continues, there is little doubt that before the century has run its course Sikh religion will have become a branch of Hinduism and the Sikhs a part of the Hindu social system."[1] But orthodox Sikhs strongly repudiate this opinion, and there is a revived Sikh communal movement.

HINDU RELIGIOUS LIFE

From the historical we turn to the modern, and try to give a brief sketch of the medley of religious life in India to-day.

Congregational worship of the Christian and Muslim kind is foreign to Hinduism, except for the hymn-singing of Bhakti or modern groups, and the great occasional festivals of the temples. Domestic worship in Hindu houses may take place in a prayer-room which may contain images or symbols of gods. The image may be in human form, and washed, dressed, and fed as in ancient Egypt. Or it may be a simple stone, the *lingam* in the worship of Śiva. Flowers are frequently offered, and lamps lit, and sacred sentences (*mantras*) recited.

A devout Brahmin will spend a great deal of time in complicated ritual and in scripture reading and recitation. There are many other holy men, teachers (*gurus*), wandering ascetics (*sadhus*), down to the vulgar exorcists.

There are immense Hindu stone temples in India, especially in the south. Some of the northern temples were destroyed by Islam. Many of the existing temples date from recent centuries, and modern ones are being built. Most people do not go to the temples often, once or twice a year, but will make gifts at local and village shrines regularly or in time of need.

There are numerous religious festivals, with processions in bright clothing, offerings at the shrines, and general rejoicing. The magnificent temple of Jagannatha (Juggernaut) at Puri,

[1] K. Singh, *The Sikhs*, p. 185.

dedicated to Vishnu, came into disrepute with the British because of the extremes to which devotees went, throwing themselves under the wheels of the car when the god was brought out in procession. When Nanak went to the evening worship at Jagannath and was asked to take part in the offering of lights and flowers, incense and pearls, he burst out: "The sun and moon, O Lord, are thy lamps, the firmament thy salver and the orbs of the stars the pearls set therein."

Europeans were also shocked at the worship in the Kalighat at Calcutta, where, before the black gaping-mouthed figure of Kali, adorned with skulls, goats are beheaded and blood spattered around. But most Hindu worship is non-sacrificial, an offering of flowers and fruit. As the Gita says, "If one of earnest spirit set before me with devotion a leaf, a flower, a fruit, or water, I enjoy this offering of devotion."

In Hinduism there has always been respect for the powers of nature and life in all its forms. In a religion which has so long a history, and embraces so many different cults, differences of worship must be expected. The worship of the female principle in nature is expressed in manuals of ritual and magic called Tantras (Sanskrit *tantra*, thread, fundamental doctrine). In these manuals, and in paintings in some temples, representations of sexuality are said to symbolize the process by which the universe was born.

Nature-worship is found in many villages, most of whose inhabitants seem ignorant of the great gods. Snakes and other animals, and spirits of disease, sometimes connected with Kali, are worshipped in many places. The cow is sacred for Hindus, and Gandhi said that "cow-protection is the dearest possession of the Hindu heart". In this respect for animal life, many Indians, and especially the Jains and those influenced by them, have much to teach other nations.

Vows and pilgrimages are common in Hinduism, as in most other religions. Great crowds undertake the long and dusty journey to bathe in the sacred waters of the Ganges at Benares and other places. The source of the Ganges is a great place of pilgrimage, to visit which obtains great merit; and to die on the river banks is the aim of thousands. Many ascetics are seen at these places, some of them lifelong Yogis, and others who have a temporary vocation. The Yogis may be of many types, holding various religious beliefs and practices. Many are followers of Śiva, the reputed inventor of Yoga.

In the many Indian beliefs and diverse cults we are reminded again that Hinduism is the product of an agelong growth. Despite its many teachers, there never has been a reformer accepted as authoritative for the whole religious complex, such as Islam has in Muhammad. Moreover the tolerance of Hinduism allows it still to present the most diverse facets. Reforms of modern times have tried to remove those elements of worship or social organization which offend the modern mind, and which have become especially visible in the contact with other religions and cultures. But the diversity of Hinduism remains, at once attractive and baffling.

MODERN MOVEMENTS

There is no space to say more than a few words about modern movements in Hinduism, and the situation is constantly changing. The most important influences on Indian life in the last two centuries, of course, have been the coming of European commerce, government, and Christianity. There have been Syrian Christian churches in South India since the fourth century, if not from the time of the apostle Thomas, the reputed founder. These are still among the largest Indian Christian communities, and Christianity is the oldest of the non-Hindu religions in India. There have been many other Christian missions in modern times, and there are over eight million Christians in the Indian sub-continent.

Apart from the conversion of some millions of Indians to Christianity, the impact of the West has caused a revival of Hinduism. In 1828 the Brahmo-Samaj (society of believers in one Deity) was founded, with the aim of providing common ground for believers in a single God. Much more influential was the Arya-Samaj in 1875, which not only sought to revive the ancient Vedic religion but also gave some recognition to caste, karma, and the Yoga philosophy. In addition, it established missionary colleges and orphanages. To-day the

Arya-Samaj is militant in reviving Hindu faith and combating other religions. It and the Hindu Mahasabha "purify" those brought back from other religions.

Many other movements and thinkers have sought to revive the best in the past, to combat evils such as caste-discrimination, and yet to remain Hindu. Mahatma Gandhi tackled the problem of the outcastes and got many temples opened to them which had been closed previously. But caste is a deeply rooted institution. There are hundreds of castes, developed far beyond the few divisions of Aryan days, in fact representing ancient religious and social differences. A Hindu must perform his caste duty. On the other hand, opposition to caste has been an attraction of Islam.

Another religious revival, the Ramakrishna Mission, has not only sought to return to the Vedanta but also to spread this faith overseas. It is an educational and missionary body which has branches in Europe and America. Some Europeans have sought to revive the Vedanta for the West, notably the Theosophical societies. Such people too often seem not to realize the full implications of the doctrines they so easily accept. Moreover they tend to react strongly against their own religious heritage in a way that they would reprobate if they were Hindus by birth.

Mahatma Gandhi has undoubtedly been the most outstanding representative of modern India to the outside world. He freely acknowledged his debt to the West and to Christian teaching, especially the Sermon on the Mount. More than any other reformer he set himself out to effect social changes, working at removing the root of village poverty in the revival of local industry. His policy of non-violence and passive resistance owed much both to Jainism and to Christianity. But he remained a Hindu in his renunciation of the world and ideal of celibacy or married chastity. His opposition to medicine was relaxed in some measure towards the end of his life.

To-day Professor S. Radhakrishnan is one of the foremost ambassadors of Indian culture. Being well-read in Western philosophy and Christian theology, he suggests many parallels between Hindu and Christian belief. But it is difficult to fit together, for example, such diverse conceptions as the Christian teaching of forgiveness with the Indian doctrine of identity with Brahman. Rather than attempt a synthesis, it would seem better to study one another's position, recognizing differences as well as similarities.

The Bhakti tradition is continued most notably by the writings of Rabindranath Tagore (1861–1941). He interpreted the Brahmanic view of the universe as a "play", in a quite new and positive way. His devotional writings appeal to East and West. In his Gitanjali (song-offerings) he is close to the ancient mystics, especially Kabir.

"Thou hast made me endless, such is thy pleasure. This frail vessel thou emptiest again and again, and fillest it ever with fresh life."

In Tagore, too, there is the mystical revolt against formalism and a clear recognition that deliverance is not by escape from the world but by dedication in the world.

"Leave this chanting and singing and telling of beads! Whom dost thou worship in this lonely dark corner of a temple with all doors shut? Open thine eyes and see thy God is not before thee!
He is there where the tiller is tilling the hard ground and where the path-maker is breaking stones."

And there is deep concern for the poor and needy as belonging to God.

"Here is thy footstool and there rest thy feet where live the poorest, and lowliest, and lost.
When I try to bow to thee, my obeisance cannot reach down to the depth where thy feet rest among the poorest, and lowliest, and lost."[1]

NOTE ON THE PARSIS

The Parsis (Persians) are the modern followers of the ancient religion of Zarathustra (Zoroaster), who lived centuries ago in Persia. To-day most of the small number who remain

[1] R. Tagore, *Gitanjali*, pp. 1, 8–9.

faithful to this ancient faith are found in India, in the district of Bombay. Their number is estimated at only 114,000, one of the smallest religious minorities of India, but they are important for their religion, wealth, and social activities.

Zarathustra is said to have lived in Persia about 660–583 B.C., though some scholars think that his dates should be put earlier. Legend later attributed to his mother a miraculous conception, and to himself temptations by the spirit of evil, Angra Mainyu. The Persians of his day were mostly Aryans like their Indian neighbours, and worshipped similar gods, Mitra, Varuna, and Indra. Zarathustra was a reformer like Muhammad, who urged his people to give up the worship of the lower gods and be faithful to Ahura Mazda ("the wise Lord", also called Ormuzd). The teaching of Zarathustra is a clear monotheism and it has been thought to have influenced the Jews in their exile and subjection to the Persian empire. There is a dualism of the God of good and the evil spirit, but it is questioned whether this is complete dualism, and the good God has final power.

The Parsi scriptures are called the Avesta, and embedded in the liturgical matter are the Hymns (Gathas) of Zarathustra, which are remarkable for their lofty teaching. Judgement and a future life are taught here, the latter more clearly than in most of the Old Testament.

Zoroastrianism became the religion of the Persian state, and later fell into decline. The Magi of Greek and Christian literature were astrologers who seem to have known or understood little of the Avesta. After the coming of Islam to Persia in A.D. 639 persecution arose, and finally most of those who clung to their ancient faith migrated to India.

The Parsi fire-temples have become known to the West. They are simple buildings, without images or pictures, and fire is kept burning in a metal vase on the altar. Devout Parsis pray to Ahura Mazda before the fire, and bring offerings of bread, water, and sacred drink (*haoma*). Prayers are also said in the open, facing the setting sun. The dead are not buried or cremated, but put on shelves in round "Towers of Silence". where the vultures pick the bones clean.

Parsis became affected by Hindu practices: e.g. hereditary priesthood, child marriage, formal ritual. But they rejected reincarnation and some other Hindu beliefs. After contact with Europeans, there began reform movements to remove the accretions of centuries and to return to the neglected Gathas. The Parsis to-day have been some of the leaders of business, and of education and social reform.

Short Bibliography

A. C. Bouquet, *Hinduism* (Hutchinson)

E. H. Smith, *Outline of Hinduism* (Epworth)

J. W. Waterhouse, *Zoroastrianism* (Epworth)

D. Field, *The Religion of the Sikhs* (Murray)

S. Piggott, *Prehistoric India* (Pelican)

N. Macnicol, *Hindu Scriptures* (Everyman)

E. J. Thomas, *Vedic Hymns* (Murray)

——, *The Song of the Lord* (Murray)

L. D. Barnett, *Brahma-Knowledge* (Murray)

J. D. Guillemin, *The Hymns of Zarathustra* (Murray)

R. C. Zaehner, *The Teachings of the Magi* (Allen & Unwin)

A. J. Appasamy, *Temple Bells* (Student Christian Movement)

R. Tagore, *Gitanjali* (Macmillan)

——, *Sadhana, the Realisation of Life* (Macmillan)

T. Singh, *Sikhism,* (Orient Longmans)

S. Radhakrishnan, *The Hindu View of Life* (Allen & Unwin)

4

Buddhism

BACKGROUND AND SOURCES

BUDDHISM is the link between India and the rest of Asia, the transmitter of Indian culture. Buddhism did not survive in India but, as Hinduism was a national religion, so Buddhism became a missionary faith to other lands.

Like Christianity and Islam, Buddhism had a historical founder, Gotama. Practically all the traditional details of his life have been questioned, but there is little doubt that he was a historical teacher. Like many another wandering philosopher of his time, Gotama set out his own interpretation of the problems that were exercising men's minds. So Buddhism, like other historical religions, built on ancient foundations and reformed a good deal that was considered unnecessary and deluding.

The modern province of Bihar in eastern India where Gotama lived seems hardly to have come under the influence of the Brahmins in the sixth century B.C., though their authority was strong to the west. The teachers of Bihar were mostly of the warrior caste, like Mahavira the historical founder of Jainism and Gotama himself. These were not the first teachers, for it is said that there were previous Buddhas before Gotama and some twenty Jinas before Mahavira. Something of the climate of thought prevailing at the time of the rise of Jainism and Buddhism has been mentioned in the previous chapter on Hinduism.

It is exceedingly difficult to sort out the facts of the life of Gotama, from the mass of legend and romance with which later devotion embellished it. Believers accept all the traditional details and teaching as original. In modern times European scholars have worked on the records which are far harder to unravel, and much further distant from the life that they adorn, than are the Christian Gospels for the life of Jesus.

Some of the most important scriptures for our purpose are preserved in Ceylon, Burma, and Siam in a dialect of Sanskrit known as Pali. It seems that Gotama did not speak Pali, but it arose later as one of the chief literary languages of Buddhism. These Pali works, monastic rules (Vinaya) and sermons (Suttas), relate circumstances of Gotama's life in which sermons were preached and rules laid down. The Pali scriptures have come to us in palm-leaf books based on originals of about the first century B.C. There were earlier scriptures said to have existed at the time of the Third Buddhist Council in 247 B.C., held some 230 years after the death of Gotama. But there were numerous sects, with their own differing scriptures.

Other forms of tradition existed in Sanskrit, of which there are translations and fragments existing in Chinese and Tibetan. Later Sanskrit works give much expanded stories of the Buddha, but show signs of being based on older originals.

Early English accounts of Buddhism (such as Sir Edwin Arnold's *Light of Asia*, 1879) were based on Sanskrit translations. Pali only became known to the West after 1870, but then the Pali texts were felt to give an earlier and more reliable tradition. More material has become available in this century, with translations from Chinese and Tibetan, but these are largely of legendary character.

The Pali scriptures are about twice as long as the Bible. They are in three main collections, called Three Baskets (Tipitaka; Tripitaka in Sanskrit). The Vinaya Pitaka (Discipline Basket) gives rules for monks. The Sutta Pitaka (Discourse Basket) gives statements of faith and dialogues of Gotama's teaching. There is often attached to it the most famous of Buddhist works, the Dhammapada, the "Way of Virtue", a beautiful collection of poetry. The Abhidhamma

Pitaka (Metaphysical Basket) is a more advanced manual for monks.

There is also a collection of stories, the Jataka, Birth Tales, giving popular beliefs about the 550 previous births of the Buddha, which reflect ancient Indian thought. Not in the canon of scripture, but of some interest is the book called *The Questions of King Milinda*. This is a collection of dialogues purporting to have taken place between a Buddhist sage and the Greek king Menander.

THE LIFE OF GOTAMA

The Buddhist scriptures do not attempt a continuous biography of Gotama. Events are mentioned to illustrate his teaching. It is thought that he was born about 563 B.C. and died in 483 B.C. Some scholars would put his dates rather earlier.

Gotama (in Pali; Gautama in Sanskrit) was the family name. The boy's personal name Siddhattha (or Siddhartha) is rarely used. He belonged to the clan of the Sakyas, and in China he is often called Sakyamuni, the sage of the Sakyas.

Gotama's father was Suddhodana and his mother Maya. The country of the Sakyas was along the southern frontiers of Nepal. Its capital, Kapilavatthu, was long a place of Buddhist pilgrimage. In 1896 was discovered a memorial stone set up by the emperor Aśoka (third century B.C.) in the Lumbini Park to show that "the Blessed One was born here".

The legends say that Gotama's father was a great king, and that his son could have been a universal monarch. But it seems that he was raja of a small tribe whose chief occupation was the cultivation of rice. According to the popular Sanskrit stories, Gotama in heaven resolved to become a Buddha and chose the place of his last rebirth. When he descended into his mother's womb the whole universe shook and four gods came to protect his mother. The best known legend says that he became a white elephant, smote his mother's right side and appeared to enter her womb. As soon as he was born he stood on his feet, took seven long steps, surveyed all the world, and declared himself the chief of all. Such narratives, like the Apocryphal Gospels, do not need to be taken historically. The older accounts suggest nothing abnormal in Gotama's birth.

Gotama was brought up in comfort, married a girl called Yaśodhara (the name varies in different sources), and had a son named Rahula. Gotama was a thoughtful boy, and he was dissatisfied with the things of this world. Legends say that sages and Brahmins prophesied great things for him: that he would either become a universal ruler, or else a fully enlightened Buddha. They told his father that Gotama would renounce the world when he had seen four signs: an old man, a sick man, a corpse, and an ascetic. So his father had guards stationed all round his palace, to prevent the boy going outside to where he might see these signs of disease and death.

The earlier version of this story seems to have been simply an account of Gotama's thoughts on the subject of sickness and sorrow. "There came to me the thought. . . . Being myself subject to decay, disease, death, sorrow, and the impurities, and seeing the disadvantage (of what is subject to these things), what if I were to search after the untainted, unsurpassed, perfect security, which is Nirvana?"[1]

It is said that at the age of twenty-nine Gotama gave up his home life in a Great Renunciation. His wife had just given birth to a son, and it seems that Gotama regarded this as a further bond to tie him to home. So he crept out at night and left his home for ever. This sort of renunciation was typical of the age, and one who would fathom spiritual reality often felt obliged to give up all earthly ties.

The legends delight in telling how Gotama left the city on a horse, vanquished the efforts of the tempter Mara to restrain him in earthly comforts, galloped on in the company of gods, and when he left his horse it died of a broken heart and was reborn as a god. The Pali scriptures are much more restrained: "When I was a young lad, a black-haired stripling, endowed with a happy youth, in the first flush of manhood, against my mother's and my father's wish, who lamented with tearful eyes, I had the hair of head and face shaved off,

[1] F. L. Woodward, *Some Sayings of the Buddha*, pp. 1–2.

I donned the saffron robes, and I went forth from my home to the homeless life."[1]

In his search for spiritual enlightenment, Gotama tried the various methods of discipline current in his day. First he became the disciple of a teacher of Yoga meditation. But he found it brought him to a state of nothingness rather than peace. "This doctrine extending to the attainment of the state of Nothingness does not conduce to aversion, absence of passion, tranquillity, higher knowledge, Nirvana. So without tending this doctrine I abandoned it in disgust."[2]

Then he tried extreme self-mortification and fasting, like the Jains. He persevered until, "as the beams of an old shed stick out, so did my ribs stick out through little food. . . . When I thought I would touch the skin of my stomach, I actually took hold of my spine." Five wandering ascetics were attracted to him by his harsh discipline, feeling that new revelation would come in this way.

But Gotama still found no enlightenment. "Then I thought, it is not easy to gain that happy state while my body is so very lean. What if I now take solid food, rice and sour milk." He acted upon this wise thought, and strengthened himself. But the ascetics now regarded him as an impostor and left him in disgust.

Fortified and purified, Gotama came to Uruvela, a pleasant spot on the banks of a river. Tradition says that he sat down under a tree, the Tree of Enlightenment (Bodhi or Bo-tree), until peace should come. Here he concentrated his mind on the passing away and rebirth of beings, and on the destruction of desire. Finally came the light. "I did attain unto the utter peace of Nirvana that is free from the impurities, so that the Knowledge arose in me, the Insight arose in me thus: Sure is my release. This is my last birth. There is no more birth for me." So he became Buddha, the Enlightened One.

On the traditional site of the Enlightenment, at Buddha Gaya in Bihar, stands to-day a great temple to which pilgrims come from all parts of the Buddhist world. It is under Hindu

[1] Woodward, p. 2.
[2] E. J. Thomas, *The Life of Buddha*, pp. 63f.

66

control. But at Sarnath near Benares is the Buddhist-controlled centre in the Deer Park where the Buddha preached his first sermon.

Legends say that Buddha had to struggle with the evil Mara, and that when he overcame him all the gods shouted for joy. Then Buddha hesitated about declaring his doctrine, but the god Brahman pleaded with him saying, "There are beings of little impurity that are falling away through not hearing the doctrine."

Finally Gotama decided to preach to the five ascetics who had left him and he made his way towards Benares. When they saw him coming they determined not to give him respect, since Gotama had abandoned asceticism. This was a critical moment. Would the Buddha be given a hearing? But when they met him the monks were not able to withhold their respect, and Buddha preached his first sermon, "Setting in motion the Wheel of the Law."

There is a traditional version of this sermon. It teaches the Middle Way, between the extremes of passion and self-torture, it teaches the Noble Eightfold Path (see later), the truths of the cause of pain and the cessation of pain, the non-existence of the soul, and the attainment of the highest complete enlightenment.

There is no connected account of the life of the Buddha, and it is even less possible to work out the chronology of the long period between his Enlightenment and his death. The Great Renunciation took place about 534 B.C. and the Enlightenment in 528. There remained about forty-five years of teaching and travelling until his death about 483.

The five mendicants were converted and became Arahats (worthy ones), having broken the fetters of the passions, and having attained Nirvana, like the Buddha, they would not have to be reborn. Other converts came in soon, bringing the total up to sixty. They formed a community (sangha), living in retreat, and learning the doctrine during the three months' rainy season, and going out begging and teaching for the rest of the year. Many rich people became interested in the movement, for Gotama himself was of noble blood, and they gave fine parks for the monks to rest in. One of his most notable converts was King Bimbisara of Rajagaha.

Buddha seems to have visited his home early in his ministry, though the visit is not recorded in the Pali canon. His father is said to have bowed at his feet and to have been horrified when Gotama went out begging with his bowl, according to the rules of his order. His son Rahula became a monk, but was not prominent among his followers. When Rahula joined the order Gotama's father came to request that a son should not be ordained without the permission of his father and mother. Hostility had grown up among the people of the country because, by attracting young men as monks, Gotama was accused of breaking up families and producing widows and childlessness.

The most important figure among the monks was Ananda, who devoted himself to the care of the Buddha. But the ancient records give no account of Ananda's conversion, nor yet of that of another monk, Devadatta, who tried to harm and disparage the Buddha.

Gotama's aunt was admitted to the order, at the entreaty of Ananda. Thus she became the first nun. The Buddha's reluctance to admit her and remarks on the admission of women will be mentioned later. But it is clear that women played a fair part in the movement, by ministering to its needs in food and clothing. The part taken by the laity will also be referred to later.

In approximately 483 B.C. (according to most European scholars) came the Buddha's death, or entry into Nirvana. Tradition gives considerable details, some more reliable than others. In one account the tempter Mara was with him to the end. More probable are the stories of the human distress of Ananda and other disciples.

At the beginning of the rainy season strong pains came upon Gotama and grievous sickness. Ananda seeing this begged his master to give some authoritative instructions for his monks. But the Buddha protested that there was no secret doctrine : "I have taught you the Norm, Ananda, by making it without inner or outer. There is no closed fist of the teacher."

Then a metal-worker named Chunda prepared a choice meal of hogsflesh and put it in Gotama's bowl. The Buddha told him to bury the rest in the ground, for neither gods nor men could digest it. The food brought on violent pains and dysentery, but Gotama sent word to Chunda not to feel remorse and managed to continue his journey to Kusinara. It should be noted that although the Buddha forbade the taking of life, yet he would eat meat if it was offered in charity. Many Buddhists to-day are not strict vegetarians.

At Kusinara, a small capital town, Gotama lay down in a grove and gave final talks to his monks. Ananda was weeping, but the Buddha called him and said, "Sorrow not, lament not! Have I not said to you ere now, Ananda, 'In all things dear and delightful there is the element of change, of separation, of otherness.'" Because of his devoted service Ananda was promised early perfection.

The disciples were told that when the Master had gone the Doctrine would still be there. "It may be, Ananda, that you will say, gone is the word of the Master! We have no longer any Master now! But you must not so regard it, Ananda; for the Norm and Discipline taught and enjoined by me, they shall be your teachers when I am gone."[1]

Then came the words, "'Come now, brethren, I do remind ye: The elements of being are transitory. Strive earnestly.' These were the last words of the Exalted One."

The body of Gotama was cremated, according to Hindu custom. The bones are said to have been taken as relics. One of the teeth is believed to be now in the famous Temple of the Tooth at Kandy, Ceylon. In 1898 a stone vessel, containing fragments of bone, was discovered near the Nepalese frontier which from the inscription seems to be a relic-treasury of the Buddha and the Sakyas, and to date from the period of King Aśoka. Stupas (monuments) for containing relics are found in many other places. Whether these are genuine relics or not, they do show that the Buddha was regarded as a man and not an unhistorical figure like Rama or Krishna.

---

[1] Woodward, pp. 349, 354.

THE DOCTRINE (DHAMMA)

At the beginning of every Buddhist meeting is recited the threefold formula:

> I go to the Buddha for refuge,
> I go to the Dhamma for refuge,
> I go to the Sangha for refuge.

These are the three Jewels: Buddha, Dhamma (doctrine or law), Sangha (order or community). By repeating this formula one became a member of the Buddhist faith.

The Pali word Dhamma (Sanskrit Dharma, from the root *dhri*, to establish) means, "that which is established or firm", and by extension, "custom, law, duty, doctrine, religion". The law or doctrine was the subject of the discourses of the Buddha and it enlightened the hearers.

The early Buddhist writings are predominantly intellectual. Great stress is laid upon knowledge and right understanding. There is small place for emotion, such as is often a large part of religion. Gotama spoke not to the common people so much as to struggling thinkers like himself, who had been seeking deliverance from ignorance. Hinduism, as we saw in the last chapter, developed the Bhakti cults of devotion to a personal God, partly in reaction against the intellectual systems of the day. When Buddhism developed as a popular religion, and in other lands, it took to itself new beliefs.

Gotama neither affirms nor denies the religious beliefs of his day. He mentions the gods as being subject, like men, to the law of *karma*. Against those who see in his system sheer atheism or mere ethics, some modern writers insist that Gotama and his disciples had a profound belief in the spiritual power behind nature. Mrs Rhys-Davids, a great authority, says: "The educated man in Buddha's day believed in Deity as immanent in each man, as the Most, the Highest, the Best in that man's spiritual being or self."

The Buddha was a practical teacher. In his first discourse we find the Four Noble (Aryan) Truths, his diagnosis and cure for suffering. These are: the Fact of Suffering, the Cause

70

of Suffering, the Cessation of Suffering, the Noble (Aryan) Eightfold Path.

The Fact of Universal Suffering is seen in birth, decay, sickness, and death, "In a word, this body, this fivefold mass which is based on Grasping, that is Suffering." The Cause of Suffering is the craving that leads to birth, the lust that lingers here, the desire to be reborn. The Cessation of Suffering comes by giving up and release from this craving. The way to obtain this release is by the discipline of the Noble Eightfold Path. This emphasis on universal suffering is often called pessimistic. But most Buddhists are not pessimists, and Gotama does offer a way out of suffering. He presents the facts of life as he sees them, and then shows a way of redemption.

Gotama took over from the Indian thought of his time the belief in *karma*. The craving and lusts which are not overcome in this life leave behind them a *karma* which creates a new being. So the good and evil in our minds are the result of *karma*. "Beings have their own karma, they are heirs of karma, their origin is karma, they have karma as their kinsman, as their resource. Karma distributes beings, that is, according to lowness and greatness."[1]

Buddhist teaching is distinguished from that of the Brahmins by its denial of the self or ego. We saw in the last chapter that the Upanishads taught the union of the soul (*atman*) with Brahman. The Jains denied the existence of a Supreme Being, but taught a plurality of souls. Buddhism denies that there is a permanent soul. This statement, however, needs to be qualified. Buddhism teaches that everything is relative and changing. It denies the Brahmin doctrine that there is a changeless self which merely assumes new phases like putting on clothes.

In one of his earliest teachings Gotama declares that the body is not the self, the feelings are not the self, consciousness is not the self, for if it were it would not be involved in sickness. By being disgusted with body, feelings, perception, and consciousness, a man is repelled and freed from birth and rebirth, he is liberated.

[1] E. J. Thomas, *Early Buddhist Scriptures*, p. 127.

Nevertheless there seems to be a contradiction inherent in the conjunction of the no-soul theory and karma and rebirth. If there is no soul, then how can there be rebirth? This has remained a paradox in Buddhist teaching. The "doctrine of annihilation at death was denied throughout the whole history of Buddhism. The individual being had existed before, and he would exist again. . . . His personal identity remained to such an extent that he could come to remember his former existences. . . . The question of the dissolution of personality only becomes urgent when it is asked what takes place with the cessation of rebirth. Naturally no one can give an answer to that except the one who has reached that state."[1]

In his practical way, Gotama concentrated on the way of living. Freedom of suffering comes by following the Noble Eightfold Path. This is Right View, Right Resolve, Right Speech, Right Activity, Right Livelihood, Right Endeavour, Right Mindfulness, Right Rapture.

It is easier to follow the sequence if one sees three stages in the Path. The first two articles, Right View and Right Resolve, are the result of Enlightenment; we perceive the fruits of suffering and resolve to destroy craving. The next three, Right Speech, Activity, and Livelihood, are the practice of morality, control of words, conduct, and the business of life. The last three, Right Endeavour, Mindfulness, and Rapture, refer to supernormal states. They are the last stages of mind-training, which bring lucid thought, and may lead on to ecstatic states, here linking up with Yoga practices.

By following the Noble Eightfold Path of mental training, lust is destroyed. "This is that Middle Path, which giveth vision, which giveth knowledge, which causeth calm, insight, enlightenment, and Nirvana."

Buddhist teaching might be called that of the selfless life. By its doctrine of no-self (anatta) it might seem denial of existence. But it does not state that there are not other existences, before birth and after death. It simply insists that everything is complex, compound, and transitory. This has an important bearing on the teaching of Nirvana.

[1] E. J. Thomas, The History of Buddhist Thought, p. 260.

The word *nirvana* (Pali *nibbana*) means "going out". It is clearly connected with the cessation of craving. But this does not necessarily imply annihilation. As a modern authority puts it, "Nirvana never means nullity, either to Buddhists or to other Indian thinkers . . . it means not nullity but no-thing, i.e. the indefinite." It is not a state of nothingness but indeed of activity.

The Buddha himself avoided the idea of annihilation. He taught deliverance from suffering. His monks were *arahats* (worthy ones) who had already attained Nirvana, but who remained in the world teaching the doctrine to others.

THE ORDER (SANGHA)

The third Jewel, the third Refuge of the Buddhist, was the Sangha, the Order of Community of monks. This organization has lasted from the time of the Buddha to the present day and has given permanence to his religion.

Hindu ascetics are normally individuals seeking their own salvation in solitude. Jains went about naked and often filthy, living on scraps. Buddhist monks were organized into monastic communities, dressed in yellow robes and provided with begging-bowls. The monk was called a *bhikkhu* (mendicant), and he had as sole property his robes, begging-bowl, a needle, a tool for cutting firewood, and a filter so that he might not take insect life in drinking water.

At the beginning, of course, there were few rules, but as the order grew regulations multiplied. Lands were provided for the monks by well-wishers and houses given them to live in. There were some who preferred the solitary life, but the community was the standard. There were no caste-distinctions in the order. On the other hand, Gotama was not a social reformer setting out to abolish caste altogether.

The monks were not priests, nor were they an aristocratic corporation seeking to control politics (though they became such in Tibet, for example). They did not care for such worldly things, on the whole, but sought to follow the Way and teach the Doctrine. There were no rigid vows, and the monks were always free to return to the world. So it is that in some countries, like Burma even to-day, nearly all men have been monks for shorter or longer periods. It is part of the training of youth, and of preparation for age. This allows for a high level of conduct, since there is no strained lifelong celibacy unless one prefers it.

Women were admitted to an order of female ascetics with reluctance. Gotama's aunt and foster-mother came and pleaded to be admitted as a nun and Ananda championed her cause. Eventually Gotama gave way, but he is reported to have said that the good doctrine would have lasted a thousand years, "but as women have gone forth, now the religious system will not last long, now, Ananda, the good doctrine will only last five hundred years". However his fears were not realized, and few women entered the order.

Ten precepts are given as binding on monks. "To avoid the taking of life; to avoid taking what is not given; to avoid unchastity; to avoid falsehood; to avoid fermented liquor and intoxicants giving rise to sloth; to avoid unseasonable meals; to avoid dancing, song, playing music, and seeing shows; to avoid the use of flowers, scents, and unguents, wearing ornaments and decorations; to avoid the use of raised beds and of wide beds; to avoid the accepting of gold and silver."[1]

This meant complete poverty, chastity, and sobriety, and puritanical self-denial, all with the aim of overcoming cravings. The prescribed begging-round should be made, even when food has been provided by a generous layman. The bhikkhus depended on the hospitality of the laity. Strictly speaking they were not begging, but giving the laity a chance to acquire merit by acts of charity.

The Buddhist layman seeks refuge in the Buddha, the Doctrine, and the Order, but he retains his life in the ordinary world, though he may become a monk for a time. The ten precepts were reduced to the first five for the laity, and the commandment against unchastity did not, of course, forbid marriage but infidelity. The prohibition against taking life has distinguished Buddhism in its kindness to animals and its opposition to warfare. Blood-sports, shooting, and warfare

[1] Woodward, p. 53.

are anathema to the pious Buddhist. If he does not always live up to his ideals, he is not unlike members of other faiths. To its honour, Buddhism has not (with rare exceptions) persecuted or spread its faith by the sword.

The scriptures contain some very practical advice for the layman: not to drink liquor, not to roam the streets at night, not to have evil companions, not to be given to idling. The foolishness of gambling is explained: "If one wins, he wins a foe. If he lose, he has to lament his loss. Gone is his visible means of subsistence. . . . Friends and ministers of state treat him with contempt. He is not sought after by those who give and take in marriage, for they say, 'A gambler is not competent to support a wife.'"[1]

The Dhammapada, the Way of Virtue, has always been a very popular handbook of devotion and conduct, and some of its sentences are worth quoting.

"Never does hatred cease by hating, by not hating does it cease; this is the ancient law. . . . 'He has abused me, beaten me, worsted me, robbed me', those who dwell not on such thoughts are freed of hate. . . .

Zeal is the way to Nirvana. Sloth is the day of death. The zealous die not; the slothful are as it were dead. . . .

Even the gods emulate him whose senses are quiet as horses well-tamed by the charioteer, who has renounced self-will, and put away all taints. . . .

To all life is dear. Judge then by thyself, and forbear to slay or to cause slaughter. . . .

Hurt none by word or deed, be consistent in well-doing; be moderate in food, dwell in solitude, and give yourselves to meditation—this is the teaching of Buddhas."[2]

THE GROWTH OF BUDDHISM

Our records of the first two hundred years of Buddhism are very scanty. Tradition says that on the death of the Buddha a Council, or meeting of monks, was held at Rajagaha in the rainy season to decide what rules were binding, and to

[1] Woodward, p. 152.
[2] W. D. C. Wagiswara, *The Buddha's "Way of Virtue"*.

prevent divergent opinions. The Dhamma and the Vinaya (discipline) were adopted by chanting together.

About a hundred years later another Council was held at Vesali, to meet the claims of those who wished to relax the older discipline. The claims were rejected and the Vinaya reaffirmed.

Some of the early variant doctrines were that a soul exists in the truest sense, that an arahat can fall from his state, that a god can enter the Buddhist way, and that even an unconverted man can rid himself of lust.

Differing schools sprang up, not always distinct enough to be called sects, but some with their own collections of the "scriptures". These collections had not yet been written down, but were preserved by memory, which accounts for variations.

The great landmark in the early history of Buddhism is the life and activity of the emperor Aśoka, who reigned from 274 to 232 B.C. He was the grandson of Chandragupta, who had defeated Seleucus the Greek general succeeding to Alexander the Great. Aśoka himself claims to have sent Buddhist missionaries to Antiochus and Ptolemy, in Syria and Egypt.

Aśoka started as a layman, but later joined the Order and gave himself up to the spread of religion. It is not clear whether he abdicated, but he used his great power and influence to spread Buddhism far and wide. He had become horrified by warfare, and was determined to spread peace and kindness to all living things.

Particularly valuable are the stone inscriptions which Aśoka left behind, some forty of which still exist. They contain sermons and instructions about conduct: truth-speaking, obedience to parents, reverence to teachers, respect for all living creatures. Aśoka forbade animal sacrifices (which prohibition would arouse the animosity of Brahmins), put an end to the killing of animals for food in the royal palace, and built wells and planted trees for the comfort of both man and beast. He also arranged processions to please and teach the people.

Aśoka sent missions in all directions. Nothing is known of

his embassies to Syria and Egypt, but he spread Buddhism in India from Kashmir to the mouths of the Ganges and southwards nearly as far as Madras. Most important were his missions to Ceylon which dates its conversion to the faith from Aśoka's time.

A third Council at Pataliputta is said to have been held under Aśoka, about 240 B.C., though not recorded in the monuments. Here the present Pali canon of scriptures is said to have been fixed. King Aśoka, however, was tolerant, and allowed each man to live according to his own creed. He goes down to history as one of the most humane and sincerely religious of emperors.

Dissensions had already been apparent among Buddhists before the time of Aśoka, as was inevitable in a system where there was no authoritative head. The Council of Pataliputta was recognized only by the Pali school. Even among later Pali works there appear new ideas in the "Questions of King Milinda", in which the *arahat* appears as a saviour to other people.

The great division that has split Buddhism ever since into two main camps appears clearly by the beginning of the Christian era. Mongolian peoples had established their empire over northern India, and one of their principal kings, Kanishka (first–second century A.D.), was converted to Buddhism. This was a Sanskrit Buddhism which enlarged the faith. It is said that Kanishka called a council in Kashmir at which commentaries embodying the ideas of a modified Buddhism were accepted. This council was not recognized by the Pali school.

The schism is now between the narrower Hinayana or Pali Buddhists of the south, and the broader Mahayana northern Buddhists. The origin of the terms Hinayana and Mahayana is not certain. *Yana* means a vehicle, or method of transport, *maha* means great and *hina* small. The Mahayana, or "Great Vehicle", school claimed that theirs was the vehicle to universal salvation, large enough for all mankind. They called the others Hinayana, Lesser Vehicle, as a term of reproach. The Hinayanists call themselves Theravadins, followers of the Doctrine of the Elders.

From this time onwards the whole of Buddhism is split between Mahayana and Hinayana. The Mahayana spread first in north-western India and then in China, Tibet, Korea, and Japan. The Hinayana, Pali or Southern Buddhism as it is also called, spread into Ceylon, Burma, Siam (Thailand), and south-east Asia.

There is no doubt that the Hinayana school has kept itself more free from later accretion than has the Mahayana. The latter has won its way by allowing doctrines and practices that appeal to the masses, and by adopting religious beliefs of the lands into which it has spread. Some modern scholars, however, dispute the claims of Hinayana to represent correctly the original teaching of the Buddha. The accepted Pali canon was only one among a number of versions of Gotama's teaching. Moreover, there are signs that on some important matters, such as the no-soul doctrine, Gotama was more reticent than later Hinayana theologians have been. It may well be that the Mahayana school, despite its other accretions, has retained something of the more positive character of the Buddha's teaching.

BUDDHISM IN CEYLON, BURMA, AND SOUTH-EAST ASIA

We shall now give a sketch of the Buddhism of the Hinayana countries, of Pali or Southern Buddhism. A study of the Mahayana lands will come later under the religions of China and Japan.

Hinayana Buddhism is sometimes called Sinhalese (of Ceylon) because it ceased to exist in India, and both Burma and Siam accepted the authority of Ceylon. But it did not originate in Ceylon. We have seen that Aśoka sent missionaries to Ceylon, and the Buddhist church there accepts this as its traditional founding.

Ceylon seems to have accepted the faith rapidly, and later missions from India were said to have brought a branch of the sacred Bo-tree under which the Buddha gained enlightenment, and his alms-bowl. The latter had adventures comparable to those of the Holy Grail in Christian legend. The sacred tooth of the Buddha also suffered in struggles down the ages. When the Portuguese arrived in Ceylon in 1505 they seized the tooth and, despite an enormous ransom which was offered for it, they pounded it to pieces, burnt the fragments, and scattered the ashes over the sea. But Buddhists say this was not the true tooth, which is enshrined in a golden lotus and jewelled cases in the temple at Kandy.

There is no need here to trace the history of Buddhism in Ceylon. Mention should be made of Buddhaghośa, a great writer of the fifth century A.D. who did a great deal for the Hinayana school, by interpreting terms and ideas, and illustrating them with stories and legends.

Although Buddhism in Ceylon claims to be superior in purity to the Mahayana, yet there are many accretions that have found their way into the religion. There are many stupas (dagobas), buildings containing relics, and this veneration of relics is like the saint-worship of other countries and is a significant part of the religion.

Buddhism in Ceylon exists alongside other religious beliefs and gods. Some of the gods are Hindu and others are of the ancient religion of the country (Kapuism). Near the Temple of the Tooth are four temples of other gods which are maintained and used by Buddhists. One of these is to Vishnu, and most Buddhist temples in Ceylon have a room with an image of Vishnu. Many other lesser gods are worshipped.

Buddhist monasteries in Ceylon are often small, or in the country away from the people. It seems that the abstract teaching of the monks has little hold on the life of the masses. Popular religion gives great place to gods and demons, the spirit-possession of whose devotees has attracted great interest. Europeans have called it "devil-dancing".

To-day there are movements for reform among the Buddhists of Ceylon, sweeping away accretions and returning to the teaching of the Pali canon. Whether this will draw the people as a whole remains to be seen.

In Burma Buddhism is much closer to the life of the people. There is a tradition that Aśoka also sent missionaries hither, but it seems more likely that the faith came later and was invigorated by Buddhaghośa. Hinayana Buddhism is at its best in Burma and it deeply affects the life of the people. Yet as they are notoriously happy folk it seems that the supposed pessimism of Buddhism can have little effect.

All over Burma there are pagodas (stupas), conical buildings to enshrine some relic or just built as works of devotion. It is the ambition of every man to be known as a pagoda-builder, and much money is sacrificed to this end. The famous Shwe-Dagon pagoda of Rangoon is covered with gold leaf, constantly renewed. It is said to enclose some hairs of Gotama and relics of three earlier Buddhas. Many images of the Buddha are to be found, often accompanied by other figures. The praises of the Buddha are recited daily with great devotion by the laity.

In addition there are thousands of monasteries, at least two for every large village. They are usually built of teak, and are supported by gifts from the laity. The monastery is also a school for the young and gives a good Pali and Burmese education. Every young man at the age of fifteen must enter a monastery for a short time so as to qualify for manhood. Even those who take up the monastic life more permanently need not remain monks for ever.

In Burma great reverence is also given to nature spirits called Nats. They are especially associated with mountains, rivers, and trees, and have little houses made for them by the people where gifts are placed. It is sometimes said that Nat-worship is the most effective form of popular religion in Burma, but others who know the country well say that the true religion is Buddhism, and that Nat-worship is a superstition with less influence over the lives of the people than the Buddha. The great care that is devoted to pagodas, images of the Buddha, and monasteries, shows that Buddhism is a living religion in Burma.

In Siam (Thailand) Buddhism is not greatly different from that of Burma, but has some features of its own. It was influenced by Hinduism until reforms in the middle ages.

The Siamese temples (*wats*) are guarded by huge carved

figures, and inside there is always a sitting figure of the Buddha crowned with a long flame-like spire. Other figures are found as well, and some Indian gods.

The monks are numerous and, as in Burma, young males have to spend some time in the monastery. The monks act both as schoolmasters and as doctors. There are two sects, one more severe than the other. Both make the daily begging-round, except on festival days.

Religious festivals are both Buddhist and Hindu. Flowers are offered to the statues of the Buddha, and at one feast his images are bathed as in Hindu cults. Priests go round the city walls to scare away evil spirits and guns are fired in the night for the same reason. Brahmin priests are still to be found. Indian mythology, such as the Ramayana, also appears in art in the temples. There is also worship of spirits (*Phis*) like the Burmese Nats.

There is considerable mythology about the Buddha in Siam. His footprint is said to be marked in a rock. A branch of the Bo-tree was imported long ago. The Buddha is not only said to have visited Siam (as the Burmese and Sinhalese claim also for their lands), but the Siamese claim to possess his grave marked by a slab of rock beneath some great trees.

Similar forms of Buddhism are found in Cambodia and Laos, although early Hinduism and Mahayana Buddhism existed there. There are numerous monasteries to which young men go. The monks are respected and act as schoolmasters. Fine images of the Buddha and other figures are also to be found there.

There are splendid monuments of the past in great pyramid temples, such as the famous ruined temples at Angkor. They are decorated with innumerable statues in which Indian themes are prominent. There are some Buddhist images, dancing figures on lotuses and great faces like those of the Buddhas of Mahayana.

Buddhist monuments are also found in Java and some of the Malay archipelago. But these lands are now Muslim, and Buddhism has practically disappeared among the native population, except in Bali. The tide of Muslim invasion flowed down through Sumatra, Malaya, and Java, carrying all before it. It seems hardly to have affected Burma, Siam, and Cambodia, where Buddhism has remained the greatest religious force.

RELIGIOUS LIFE

From the beginning, when the Buddha preached in the Deer Park at Benares, sermons have been common in Buddhist worship. Congregational services are generally held every week or fortnight. On entering the temples the people take off their shoes and sit on mats. The hands are put together, extended towards the image of the Buddha, and silent worship offered. The monks chant in a low monotone, the audience following with reverence and bowing to the floor at certain phrases. One of the monks sits cross-legged in the preacher's throne and reads from a palm-leaf manuscript. The people listen attentively and bow at the end, and when the monks have gone out the people often drink tea. Sometimes laymen and women may spend the whole of the rest-day in meditation, with a break for food.

There is no sacrificial system in Buddhism, and the few cases that have been reported of animal sacrifice are clearly against all the tradition. Gotama said, "The kind of sacrifice in which oxen are slain, goats and sheep, fowls and pigs, and various living things are killed, such a sacrifice, brahmin, accompanied with violence, I do not praise."[1] This was a great blow to the sacrificial system of the Brahmins.

In Buddhist worship flowers are laid before the image of the Buddha and candles may be offered. People kneel in front of images or pagodas moving their lips in repetition. Others sit in rest-houses in meditation, while monks and children chant the scriptures in the monasteries.

Some have said that this is repetition but not prayer. Yet people do pray. One writer on Burma said, "I remember standing once on the platform of a famous pagoda, the golden spire rising before us, and carved shrines around us.

[1] *Early Buddhist Scriptures*, p. 186.

and seeing a woman lying there, her face to the pagoda. She was praying fervently, so fervently that her words could be heard, for she had no care for anyone about, in such trouble was she: and what she was asking was this, that her child, her baby, might not die. . . . Women often pray, I think—they pray that their husbands and those they love may be well."[1]

In the rainy season it has always been the tradition in Buddhist lands to retire to the monasteries for teaching and meditation. Little work can be done in this season and the laity as well as the monks live abstemious lives, not eating before midday. There are no plays and no marriages at this season. At the end of the rains are great festivals, especially in Burma at the great pagodas, like the Shwe Dagon. The feast lasts seven days, of which the day of the full moon is the greatest. Special offerings are brought to the monks, and the pagodas are lit with thousands of little lights so that they shine through the night like pyramids of flame.

The Buddha hardly seems to have thought that his doctrine would replace the normal popular religious festivals. Perhaps one reason why Buddhism disappeared from India was that the Brahmins were called in for family festivals and funerals. So in China the Taoist priests were called upon for family and magical needs. But even in the Hinayana lands, the great festivals, though they may not have any clear connexion with Buddhism, are yet truly religious rites, their centre in the pagoda or temple. Pilgrimages and prayers are made and great crowds assemble.

HINAYANA RELIGION

Is it a religion? This is the question that has sometimes been asked of Hinayana Buddhism. It is clear that the Mahayana enlarged itself to embrace more personal cults, but what of the Hinayana? Dr Radhakrishnan, the Indian writer, says this, "A cold, passionless metaphysic devoid of religious teaching could not long inspire enthusiasm and joy. The Hinayana ignored the groping of the spirit of man after something higher

[1] H. Fielding-Hall, *The Soul of a People*, pp. 149-50.

and wronged the spiritual side of man. The philosophical atheism of the Hinayana is the skeleton in the box."[1]

Against this the Hinayanist stresses the moral effort which Hinayana demands, against the easy faith of the Mahayana. "With the expansion of Theravada to Mahayana the tension for the individual slackened. 'Right Effort' came to imply very little effort. It is far easier to feel pleasantly benevolent to all creatures than to work for the eradication of hatred, lust, and illusion from one's own very human mind."[2]

But a number of modern writers insist that Hinayana is a full religion in its own right. An English scholar, from long residence in Burma, has recently insisted that in the conception of Nirvana there is deep religious significance as an inspiration and a goal of effort. "Nirvana is the Gospel of Buddhism. It is the term which turns pessimism into optimism. It is the term which makes it true to say that Buddhism IS a religion—not merely an ethic or a philosophy." Nirvana gives the religious meaning to moral effort, to the Law and to the Order of monks. Since Nirvana cannot be defined by the intellect, it is an object of faith. It is known only by insight, not by thought, and so it inspires life. It is an ultimate religious term, basic to the religion of Buddhism.

Further, it can be said that the Buddha himself represents for the faithful an ultimate religious symbol. The devotion that is lavished upon the Buddha, in Hinayana as well as Mahayana countries, the innumerable statues which are the work of loving craftsmen, the constant offerings, the bowings and prayers, all point to a deep religious experience. It is true that in theory the Buddha is an example, and that the task of the faithful is the "Imitation of Buddha", but imitation turns to adoration and religious experience.

In our days there is an attempted revival of Buddhism in the Hinayana countries. One result of the impact of Christianity and Western scholarship has been to send Buddhists back to their sacred books. On the more popular side, Buddhist relics from India and Ceylon have been taken to other countries and

[1] *Indian Philosophy*, Vol. I, p. 589.
[2] C. Humphreys, *Buddhism*, p. 50.

displayed with great pomp. A Pali university, with teachers of Buddhist law, was founded in Burma in 1950. As I write (1956) the Sixth Buddhist Council is drawing to a close. This is only the sixth general council to be recognized by the Hinayanists since the Buddha's death. In Rangoon a great new World Peace Pagoda has been built. A nearby cave hall, to seat 15,000 people, is banked with stone to resemble the cave in which the first Council was held at Rajagaha.

The work of the Council is to re-edit and translate the manuscripts of the Tipitaka (the Three Baskets). At the last Council in 1871 the Pali texts were transcribed from palm leaves on to marble slabs. Now the variations in differing manuscripts will be harmonized and an official version issued. Then an abridged Pali text and numerous modern translations will be made. Hundreds of monks and laymen are taking part in this work, which has been spread over two years.

According to some reckonings, the full moon day of May 1956 is 2,500 years after the death of Gotama. This is said to bring an end to the Buddhist era. There are those who believe that a new Buddha will appear. The members of the Council are seeking "to revitalize Buddhism and to prepare for its growth and expansion throughout the whole world".

It is significant that some Buddhists have recognized in Communism an enemy to Buddhism, as to all religion. Communism played an important part in the struggle for independence in Burma, but since self-government was attained many have realized that Communism is materialistic and against the religious heritage of Burma. The Premier of Burma has uttered warnings against those who have suggested "that Lord Buddha was a lesser man than Karl Marx".

In introducing the Sixth Buddhist Council the Premier said, "It is far from our intention to disparage in any way other religions like Mohammedanism, Hinduism, Christianity, or Spirit-worship. We have been prompted by the sole consideration to combat effectively anti-religious forces which are raising their ugly heads everywhere." Members of the Council are particularly concerned with the dangers of hatred and warfare in the modern world, and they feel that with its

85

tradition of peace Buddhism has an important role to play to-day. Hinayana Buddhism believes that it can offer a spiritual contribution to the troubles of the world and lead men into peace.

Short Bibliography

F. H. Smith, *The Buddhist Way of Life* (Hutchinson)
C. H. S. Ward, *Buddhism, Vol. I. Hinayana* (Epworth)
C. Humphreys, *Buddhism* (Pelican)
C. A. F. Rhys-Davids, *Outline of Buddhism* (Sheldon)
——, *Buddhism* (Home University Library)
D. L. Woodward, *Some Sayings of the Buddha* (Oxford)
W. D. C. Wagiswara, *The Buddha's "Way of Virtue"* (Murray)
E. J. Thomas, *Buddhist Scriptures* (Murray)
E. Beswick, *Jataka Tales* (Murray)
M. Percheron, *Buddha and Buddhism* (Longmans)

5

Chinese Religion

CHINA is a land of three religious or ethical systems, Confucianism, Taoism, and Buddhism, and an ancient nature worship. The "Three Religions" although different in origin are not mutually exclusive, and it is rare to find a person who holds to one form only and rejects the other two completely. It is commonly said, with characteristic Chinese tolerance, "the three religions are one", they are "three ways to one goal", and "all three claim to teach Tao", the way or order of the universe. There has been such mingling of ideas and practices that the background to modern Chinese religion is almost like that of the Hebrew, Mesopotamian, and Greek backgrounds to Christianity, and almost as hard to distinguish in religious life.

In China, as in India, we have the spectacle of a long and diverse religious development in which many elements are mingled. Primitive beliefs from ancient times have subsisted alongside of the later religious and ethical movements, but no reformer appears to sweep away the past, like a Muhammad or a Gotama. Buddhism itself appears in its Mahayana form, with a great increase in doctrines and objects of worship.

THE ANCIENT RELIGION

Early Chinese myths say that after the separation of heaven and earth the universe was ruled by twelve emperors of heaven, each reigning 18,000 years. Similar long periods are given to their successors, emperors of earth and mankind, and one is reminded of the longevity ascribed to the early men in the book of Genesis. Likewise the human emperors are said to have taught mankind its arts and crafts.

From the emergence of the first historic period of China, the Shang period, about 1500 B.C., we have remains which give some idea of certain religious beliefs of the time. Three-legged bronze sacrificial vessels have been excavated which are decorated with abstract and animal forms. They seem to have been used to hold food and wine for sacrifice to spirits and ancestors. Inscribed pieces of bone have been found, oracle bones, probably used in divination. The inscriptions and designs on bronzes and jade cult objects found in tombs give valuable information about the major concerns of early Chinese religion. Ancestors are honoured, spirits of the earth and elements worshipped, especially Ti or Shang-ti, of whom more later. Human sacrifice seems to have been practised.

These early people of northern China were agriculturists, and they believed in the spirits of the world of nature round about them. They came to worship Heaven and all its parts; Earth with its mountain and river spirits; the Elements, thunder and wind; the Seasons and the four quarters; and the five spirits of the House, at the doors, well, hearth, and inner court. To this day incense sticks are burnt at the doors, and the hearth has its picture of the kitchen god.

The earth was regarded as the giver of life to the crops and of fertility to mankind. A mound was raised to "the lords of the soil", in the centre of the village, and a small shrine to· these earth powers may still be seen under a tree at the entrance to a village. Spring and Autumn festivals, with ritual dances, are still performed in China, sometimes with modern political propaganda introduced into them. They are like agricultural festivals in other parts of the world.

The early emperors sacrificed to Shang-ti, the over-ruler. In the earliest divination Shang-ti was invoked, and in particular the Ti who were the deified ancestral spirits. Shang-ti was superior to the nature spirits, and some writers have identified him with the Supreme God. But a more abiding name for the supreme power was Tien, Heaven. This is not mentioned on the early oracle bones, but is common in early literature. Reference is frequently made to the deeds and the way of Heaven, "O bright and high Heaven, who enlightenest and rulest this lower world".

In later ages the emperor was called "Son of Heaven", the earthly representation of divine power. At the round white marble Altar of Heaven, to the south of Peking, the Son of Heaven offered sacrifices for the people on the night of the winter solstice. He also sacrificed on the Altar of Earth at the summer solstice, praying for good crops and also revering the imperial ancestors.

The nature gods were worshipped in the open air, or in little walled enclosures with a central stone altar. Roofed buildings and images were only slowly adopted. There were many local gods and differing religious practices.

Evil spirits were man's great enemy, against which he waged constant warfare. They afflicted him in flood, drought, earthquake, blight, and disease. Exorcists still do a great trade in combating the spirits of disease which threaten to steal away men's souls.

The spirits of the dead have always received great attention in China, and the development of the cult of the ancestors became the outstanding feature of Chinese religion. It was taken for granted that the soul lived on after death, and it was of great importance to ensure that the dead one should continue as a good spirit and not as a demon. So it became essential to perform all the ceremonial of burial, mourning, and later rites with scrupulous care so that the spirit should be at rest. In the past, women and servants were buried with great men, and many treasures, including the bronzes mentioned above, were interred also. To this day paper money and gifts are burnt for the dead.

CONFUCIUS

The Shang period was succeeded by that of the Chou about 1000 B.C. and the latter, in its western and eastern forms, lasted until 256 B.C. During the Chou Period there was great literary activity, so that it is known as the Classical Age of Chinese history.

The most important of the writings are called the Five Classics. The first four were said by tradition to have been compiled by Confucius and the fifth to be his own work. These Five Classics are: The Book of Changes, the Book of History, the Book of Poetry, the Book of Rites, and the Spring and Autumn Annals. To the Five Classics were later added the Analects of Confucius, a record of his sayings by his pupils, and the Book of Mencius, the philosopher who developed and added to the teaching of Confucius.

Kung Fu Tzu, Master Kung, or Confucius as the Jesuit missionaries latinized his name, lived from 551 to 479 B.C. He was a contemporary of Gotama the Buddha of India. The family name of Confucius was Kung, his personal name was Chiu (hill), said to have been given him because of his bulging skull, like a hill.

He was born in the state of Lu, part of what is now the province of Shantung. His father was an officer called Shu-Liang Ho. Later legends said that the child was born in a cave, whither his mother had been directed in a vision, and that dragons and spirit maidens hovered over the cave. In his childhood he is said to have delighted to set up sacrificial vessels and to imitate ceremonial gestures.

Tradition also endows Confucius with royal ancestors. But it is probable that his ancestors were impoverished aristocrats, and he himself worked for a time as a store-keeper. He seems to have been orphaned at an early age. He married at the age of nineteen, but apparently not happily. His only son, Li, does not appear much in the records but it seems that the father brought him up formally because "the superior man maintains a certain reserve towards his son".

Confucius had little money and his early struggles gave him a sympathy with common people that affected his teaching. He picked up a good education, though books were rare, and many of the reputed ancient classics were not yet written. He made a close study of tradition and ritual, both religious and secular.

After a time Confucius dedicated himself to teaching. At first his students were simply friends with whom he would talk and argue. Later he attracted disciples who became devoted to him. He is said to have gathered round him 3,000 disciples, but the Analects only mention twenty-two, and the number of pupils and the fame of the teacher have probably been much exaggerated.

This was a time of confusion in the state, and in course of time the pupils of Confucius were appointed to public office. He educated them in the principles of government, and laid great stress on virtue. Confucius himself, however, was not appointed to public office until he was fifty years old, and perhaps even then because his pupils felt that their master must be honoured. Tradition says that he was appointed magistrate and minister of crime and that he was so successful in enhancing public honesty that "lost objects were not picked up on the streets", and "the good old ceremonies for the remembrance and worship of the dead were again instituted". Neighbouring states became so jealous of the success of Lu, that they sent dancing girls and horses to distract the Duke, whereupon Confucius retired.

It seems, however, that Confucius held a merely nominal position, and had little to do with the Duke. He was soon disillusioned, and despite his increasing years he set off to seek a kingdom where he would be given real powers and a chance to put his principles into practice.

Confucius then spent thirteen years wandering about, offering his services to smaller states, but often being treated with coldness. He was accompanied by a small group of faithful disciples who recorded some of his conversations. Their master did not fail in his convictions, "Heaven has called me, and the superior man does not lose courage if the obstacles are many."

His last years were spent in editing and arranging books and music. A week's illness preceded his death, which he had anticipated. He died in the family home, in 479 B.C., and was buried on the river bank. His tomb may still be seen, a burial mound covered with plants, and a stone tablet on which is written, "Confucius, the Primal Sage". Emperors have bowed before this stone. There is a temple at his birthplace with a large figure of the sage. "Under the fringe his large dark eyes are humorous, kind, and thoughtful."[1]

The teaching of Confucius is not religious or philosophical, but social. But the system that came to be called by his name had its scriptures, its rituals, and above all its great emphasis on family religion and the cult of the ancestors.

Confucius was concerned with living in society, and he laid great stress on virtue, propriety, and ritual. "Only the virtuous are competent to love or to hate men," he said. One of his best known sayings is, "He who heard the truth in the morning might die content in the evening."

His Analects are full of wisdom, but often of an apparently pedestrian character. Yet he held the revolutionary doctrine that ministers should be chosen by their ability and virtue, and not because of their noble birth. He laid great stress on moral excellence, "It is Goodness that gives to a neighbourhood its beauty. One who is free to choose, yet does not prefer to dwell among the Good—how can he be accorded the name of wise?" And as a summary, a precept to guide daily conduct, he gave a negative form of the Golden Rule, "What I do not wish others to do to me, that also I wish not to do to them."[2]

It has been said that Confucius was only a moralist, and perhaps a sceptic. But it is clear that he accepted the religious beliefs of his day and had a keen sense of a divine commission from Heaven. He advised men to "keep aloof" from the spirits, but only in the sense of keeping from undue familiarity. "Some aspects of the traditional religion he approved and emphasized. Others he disapproved and tried either to transform or suppress. In general, however, he refrained from raising fundamental religious issues. . . . Quite clearly Confucius took an almost childlike pleasure in religious ritual as such."[3]

The most outstanding of the later Confucian teachers is Meng Ko, Master Meng, latinized as Mencius. He lived from

1 W. E. Soothill, *The Analects of Confucius.*
2 Ibid., pp. 30 and 40.
3 H. G. Creel, *Confucius, the Man and the Myth,* p. 124.

371 to 289 B.C. Like Confucius he aimed at guiding kings to govern wisely, but found that only his disciples would listen to him. He then set about developing the teaching of Confucius. Mencius also accepted the current ideas on religion, but he seems to have taken less interest in them than did Confucius. He believed strongly in the goodness of human nature, and that goodness must triumph in the end. "Man's nature is good, as water flows down." Mencius said that as water can flow uphill only by force, so man does evil only against his nature.

For a time Confucianism was not popular and had to compete with rival philosophies, Mohist and Taoist. But Confucians had always emphasized education and training, and with the advent of the Han empire (from 202 B.C.) they were the only men with the administrative experience to manage public affairs. So Confucianism came to power and it was in its own interest to elaborate the cult which centred in the emperor.

Confucianism suffered from its later popularity which obscured and distorted much of the original teaching. Temples were built for Confucius and his most famous disciples in every centre, where scholars gathered. The temples are without images, only simple memorial tablets, and are surrounded with gardens. The emperor himself sacrificed in honour of the philosopher Kung, Mencius, and other worthies.

At one period Confucius himself was called "emperor", and attempts were made to deify him. He was associated with the Buddha and Lao-Tzu in non-Confucian temples. Other beings, ancient sages and emperors, and even rain gods and earth gods, were associated with Confucian figures. But the Confucian scholars, on the whole, were against these forms of deification, and they gave Confucius the title of "Perfect Sage".

Many people have objected to Confucianism being classed as a religion. It is true that the state cult, centring in the worship of Heaven, Earth, and all the gods by the emperor, was controlled by the Confucian scholars and dominated by Confucian teaching. But to-day stress is laid on the social and ethical precepts of the original teaching of Confucius.

With the fall of the empire in 1911, Confucianism suffered a severe blow. The old examination system in the classical books had already been abolished, and now the imperial cult which had drawn strength from Confucian teaching came to an end. There was an abortive attempt under the Republic to make Confucianism the official religion of the state. It is interesting to note that the spearhead of the opposition to this move came from the Confucian scholars themselves. The attempt aroused great protest, in which Buddhists, Taoists, Muslims, and Christians joined under Confucian leadership. The other religions recognized the ethical value of the teachings of Confucius, but they declared that as a religion they could not satisfy men's needs. The project was dropped. Modern trends will be mentioned later.

THE CULT OF THE ANCESTORS

Before going on to discuss the Taoist movement, this is perhaps the best place to refer to the cult of the ancestors. This has been developed in China as nowhere else, and it is often called the "real religion of China".

Confucius realized the importance of filial piety for the stability of society. He said that children should spend three years in mourning for their departed parents. He is reported to have revived the ritual for "worship of the dead". Right at the beginning of the Analects we read, "are not filial devotion and respect for elders the very foundation of an unselfish life?".

Mencius said, "The worst form of filial impiety is not to have sons." The craving for sons rather than daughters runs through all Chinese life. When Buddhism came to China it was bitterly attacked by the Confucians because monks withdrew from social life, neglected their families, and left the tombs of their fathers untended. It is the duty of a wife to have sons, and the duty of a son is to ensure such burial for his father that he will be happy in the next life and will not trouble his surviving relatives as a ghost.

There are age-old regulations for burial and regular sacrifice to the dead. The son buys coffins for his parents at their last sickness or long before. The dead person is believed to go down to the Yellow Springs (like the Greek Styx), and his son goes to a stream to offer wine and paper money for the journey. There are sacrifices before the coffin for seven days, and relatives bring paper gifts which are burnt for the deceased.

Confucian rites are supplemented by Taoist exorcisms and Buddhist prayers for the dead, thus showing the mingling of the "three religions". Great care is taken over the day and the place for burial, to ensure good fortune. A special "wind-and-water" (*feng-shui*) expert is employed for this, even by many who profess to despise superstition.

The classical regulations prescribe five different mourning costumes. On the day of burial the coarsest cloth robes are worn by the sons, tied on with straw. The coffin is taken from the home amid clashing music, exploding firecrackers, and accompanied by banners and tablets on which the services of the deceased are written in glowing terms.

After the burial the most important thing is to set up the tablet for the deceased in his home. Scholars chant passages from the classics in front of the tablet, while Buddhist and Taoist priests intone prayers for the departed soul. Great quantities of paper clothing, bedding, and housing may be burnt in the open, for the use of the deceased in the world beyond. In the olden days slaves were killed as servants for the dead, and until recently widows have committed suicide for the same purpose.

Such ceremonies are repeated at intervals and on the birthdays of the deceased. In a family house there is a cabinet in the guest room, in which are placed the tablets of the nearest ancestors. This is the home altar around which the family worship is concentrated. Here morning and evening candles are lit, incense and paper money burnt, and food offered. Near to the tablets are often images of Buddhist and Taoist gods.

There are also annual sacrifices at the grave, at which those who could afford it built monuments and arches. In the spring all who can go home to the ancestral ceremony. The graves are repaired and decorated with strips of white paper. Libations and prayers are made, and guns and crackers let off. Smaller ceremonies may be held in the autumn.

Ancestral halls are built for the use of the whole clan, whose members share a common name and exact loyalty from those who bear it. The ancestral halls contain a roll of the members, and the tablets of the older ancestors are put there as they are replaced in homes by the tablets of the more recently dead.

In the ancestral halls the clan leaders meet, feasts are held, and matters of clan interest discussed. Twice a year each family should send two members to the gathering, in festive garments. Sacrifices of animals, food, and wine are placed on the altar. Candles and incense burn, and guns are fired. The elders invoke the spirits of the dead for protection and help to all the clan. After four or five days the rites come to an end, and the halls are deserted till the next festival.

TAOISM

After Confucius there was a great flowering of thought in China. Confucius had been mainly concerned with social, political, and ethical questions, but the deeper religious problems were left untouched. Later thinkers were led to religious and metaphysical questions. The famous Taoist classic, the Tao Te Ching, and Chuang Tzu, developed ideas that may even have been current in the time of Confucius. A fundamental belief was that of the unity and harmony of the universe and the need for man to achieve that harmony. The supreme goal was "Oneness with the Tao" (the Way, the *ao* as in *cow*). The striving of Confucianism was opposed, as the Tao must have its perfectly natural expression.

Tradition has associated the famous book, the Tao Te Ching, with a certain Lao Tzu, Master Lao, or Lao Tan. Many modern scholars consider that he had nothing to do with it, and that he is just a figure on whom the anonymous Tao Te Ching has been foisted. Nevertheless some of the traditional beliefs about Lao Tzu may be mentioned.

Lao Tzu is said to have been born in 604 B.C. This makes

him older than Confucius, and in the conflicts which later
developed between the two schools of thought much is made
by the Taoists of the subservience of Confucius to him. Lao
Tzu is said to have told Confucius, "Discard your proud airs,
it will all profit you nothing," while Confucius on his side
is made to declare obediently, "To-day I have seen Lao Tzu,
and I can only compare him with the dragon."

While the life of Confucius is fairly well documented, there
are only a few legends about Lao Tzu. He appears as a keeper
of archives, practising the Taoist virtues of self-effacement
and namelessness. When corruption and distress grew apace,
he withdrew from public life and set out on a pilgrimage to
the far west. On his way a mandarin requests him to write
down his teaching before it is lost, and so he is said to write the
Tao Te Ching, and then to disappear in a cloud for ever. This
is shown in pictures as the "ascension of Lao Tzu".

A modern point of view is that Lao Tzu is a composite
figure from at least three originals, and that the Tao Te Ching
is anonymous, the work of an unknown Quietist in the third
century B.C.[1]

Tao Te Ching means "the Book of the Way and the
Power". The word Tao is of great importance in Chinese
thought. It means truth, guide, way, and finally "the way of
the universe". It seems to precede God, or to be almost
identical with him. "Tao gave birth to the One; the One
gave birth successively to two things." In the Christian translation of St John's Gospel "Tao" is used for "the Word".
The word Te may be translated as virtue, or power.

The Tao Te Ching opens with the mystical statement of the
indescribable Tao:

> "The Way that can be told of is not an Unvarying
>   Way;
> The names that can be named are not unvarying
>   names.
> It was from the Nameless that Heaven and Earth
>   sprang."[2]

[1] A. Waley, *The Way and its Power*, p. 86.   [2] Ibid., p. 141.

The working out of Tao in life demands suppression of desire. "Only he that rids himself of desire can see the Secret Essences." Further, it demands self-negation and quietness.

> "The practice of Tao consists in 'subtracting day
> by day,
> Subtracting and yet again subtracting
> Till one has reached inactivity.
> But by this very inactivity
> Everything can be activated.'"

Because of the power of its quietness, the practice of Tao is often compared with water which always seeks the lowest place and yet benefits the "ten thousand creatures" of the earth.

> "Push far enough towards the Void,
> Hold fast enough to Quietness,
> And of the ten thousand things none but can
> be worked on by you . . .
> To be kingly is to be of heaven;
> To be of heaven is to be in Tao.
> Tao is forever and he that possesses it,
> Though his body ceases, is not destroyed."[1]

The Quietism that is taught so persuasively in the Tao Te Ching had developed in the fourth century B.C., by thinkers turning their speculations away from outward conduct to inward conscience. Mencius himself had said that the universe was "complete inside us". The Taoists regarded the Tao as both within and without, in which all opposites are blended and all contrasts harmonized.

The teaching of the Tao Te Ching has often been compared with Greek thought in its development in Neo-Platonism. Clearly it was too difficult for the masses, and when it did arrive at them it was in a form very different from early Taoism. But it did provide material for thoughtful and mystical people, and for artists too. Its teaching of simplicity and indifference has influenced many Chinese minds and it has

[1] A. Waley, *The Way and its Power*, pp. 162, 201.

well been called "one of the prime ingredients of Chinese culture".

Taoism was opposed to "all conquest by force of arms". "The Quietist does not regard weapons as lovely things. For to think them lovely means to delight in them, and to delight in them means to delight in the slaughter of men." There were links here to peace-loving Buddhism.

A famous early Taoist was Chuang Tzu (fourth–third century B.C.). He taught a mystical way in which was practised a sort of Yoga or "sitting in forgetfulness".

> "Do not listen with the mind but with the spirit. . . . The spirit is an emptiness to receive all things. Tao abides in the emptiness. . . . I have abandoned my body and discarded my knowledge, and so have become one with the Infinite."[1]

Chuang Tzu said much about the unreality of life, which he compared to a dream. "Those who dream do not know what they are dreaming. By and by comes the Great Awakening, and then we shall find out that life itself is a great dream." He had a dream that he was a butterfly, and on waking wondered which was the reality. "Am I now a butterfly dreaming that I am a Chuang Tzu?"

The history of later Taoism is obscure, and many of the texts of the transition period are yet unknown or untranslated. In the Han period the Taoist books, which gave religion a philosophical basis, came to be regarded as "Holy Books". They were recognized as abstruse works. By study of their esoteric meaning men sought to achieve occult powers, control of the forces of nature, immortality, and oneness with the Tao. The inactivity which Taoism had taught was seen as a road to obtaining power, "by this very inactivity everything can be activated". Later ages stressed the acquisition of power without following the way of self-negation.

The founder of the short-lived Chin dynasty, in the third century B.C., became interested in Taoist ideas and burnt

[1] Fung Yu-lan, *Chuang Tzu*, pp. 79f. It is not known how much was written by Chuang Tzu himself.

many of the Confucian classics. He sent an expensive expedition to the fabled islands of the eastern sea, where the pill of immortality was supposed to be found. In his time Taoist priests began to claim magical powers, the control of storms, and the secret of eternal life. They later professed to know the "wind-and-water" (*feng shui*) powers, and the Yin and Yang, the female and male, negative and positive principles of the universe.

When one became one with Tao, then life and death no longer had any significance. One became immortal and unrestricted by time and space and phenomena, just as was the Tao. Men left home to live ascetic lives, by fasting and vegetarianism, and so hoped to obtain deathless existence. Others undertook long journeys to reach the "Western Paradise", where the "Royal Mother of the West" ruled all things in perfect joy.

With the arrival of Buddhism in China (first to second centuries A.D.), Taoism found at once a powerful rival and an example to copy. As Mahayana Buddhism represented its Buddha in three persons, so Taoism came to have its Trinity, the "Three Pure Ones". By then Taoism had adopted the worship of state gods, and there was no objection to adding more divinities.

There was no mention of gods, still less of images, in the Tao Te Ching. But from that lofty nature-philosophy later Taoists descended to polytheism. Lao Tzu himself was deified in imitation of the Buddha. But as Lao Tzu was sunk in meditation two other gods were added to his rank. These were "The Precious Emperor God" or "The Jade Emperor", who lives on a jade mountain in the azure heaven and is perhaps a reflection of the early god Shang Ti, and "Honourable Tao" or "Mystic Jewel honoured of Heaven".

Then came many other gods and saints, spirits of the planets and elements, represented in the temples by huge images. There were gods of thunder and war, the Dragon King who controlled the floods that are so serious in China, gods and spirits of Hades, where the king of the underworld sat in judgement upon sinful mortals chained and guarded by demons.

Throughout its long history Taoism, in its popular forms, has been largely concerned with the search for immortality, the curing of sickness and disease, exorcism, divination, and all the paraphernalia of spells, charms, amulets, and incantations. Taoist priests came to specialize in dealing with evil spirits, by the use of noisy music and sacred formulas. The Tao Te Ching itself was credited with supernatural power, and is placed beside the sick to ward off evil spirits. Taoist priests gave up attempting to practise celibacy and lived among the people, pandering to their superstitions. Because of this degeneration some people say that true Taoism is practically defunct.

Nevertheless there always have been, even up to modern times, devout souls of great moral earnestness, devoted to the task of seeking inner peace and religious satisfaction through the study of the great Taoist classics. The famous scriptures remain and are studied. Moreover, Taoism has had a strong ethical side. It has been the inspiration of many lay religious societies, which have practised virtue, alms-giving, and asceticism. It has been behind most of the peasant secret societies.

Taoist temples may still be found, but the revolutions have destroyed much and broken up the organization. Yet despite persecution, corruption, and decline, it is probable that Taoist influence will remain. Taoist religion is far from being only a mass of superstition. Behind it lies a profound philosophy and a serious and exalted religious mysticism.

MAHAYANA OR NORTHERN BUDDHISM

Buddhism came to China in both its Hinayana and Mahayana forms, but the latter prevailed. The Mahayana or "Great Vehicle" began in India but migrated to northern lands, China, Tibet, Korea, and Japan, and eventually almost died out in the land of its birth. Hence it is called Northern Buddhism.

One of the chief points of emphasis in the Mahayana school is the ideal of the Bodhisattva (Being of Enlightenment), who defers his own final deliverance from the world in order to save other people. It was thought that the aim of personal salvation of the *arahats* (worthy ones) was self-centred. The motto of Mahayana became "the salvation of every living thing". An early scripture described it in these terms:

"Why do they 'the Bodhisattvas' undertake such infinite labour? For the good of others, because they want to become capable of pulling others out of this great flood of suffering. But what personal benefit do they find in the benefit of others? The benefit of others is their own benefit, because they desire it."[1]

This noble aim of world salvation is seen at work in the idealization of the Buddha himself, and then in the multiplication of other Buddhas. The later legendary lives of the Buddha delight to depict his passing through previous incarnations and renunciations, the final aim of which is his ability to appear as a saviour of mankind. Buddhism has always been concerned with the problem of suffering, and now suffering is undertaken with the clear purpose of delivering others. "Let me be glad of a suffering that redeems the world from suffering."

The Bodhisattva belief implies the conviction that merit can be transferred from one person to another, although this is against the old conception of *karma*. "I wish to be an inexhaustible treasure to the poor, a servant who furnishes them with all they lack. My life, and all my re-births, all my possessions, all the merit that I have acquired or will acquire, all that I abandon without hope of any gain for myself in order that the salvation of all beings might be promoted."[2]

From the Buddha glorified there develops the belief in worshipful beings who had been on earth in a legendary past and now appear as saviours. So the Mahayana pantheon grew up. One of these saviours is Amitabha or Amitayus ("Measureless Light" or "Life"). He is perhaps a god from Persia, especially as he is Lord of the Western Paradise (a Persian conception). This idea became popular in China.

[1] E. Conze, *Buddhism*, p. 126.   [2] Ibid., p. 149.

Then there is Avalokiteśvara ("The Lord who is looked at", or "who looks down") who is a "Lord of compassionate glances". In China he becomes the female Kwan-yin, the "Goddess of Mercy", and in Japan Kwannon, "Lord of Mercy". Finally we may mention here Maitreya (perhaps from the Vedic Mitra), the "Buddha who is to come", the personification of goodwill.

China is not so isolated from the rest of the world as it might appear to be, but until the coming of Buddhism Chinese thought was peculiarly its own. With the advent of Buddhism the world came to be looked at in new ways in China, whether men accepted Buddhism or not.

The traditional story is that the emperor Ming Ti, about A.D. 60, had a dream in which he saw a golden figure flying down from heaven and hovering over the royal palace. He was greatly frightened, but was told that it was the shining god Buddha of India. Whereupon Ming Ti sent a deputation to India to gain information about this god. It seems likely that some news about Buddhism and its fine images reached China about this time. It is said that Buddhist relics and literature were fetched from India and that two monks came with them and built the first Chinese Buddhist temple in the year 67.

Buddhist literature and priests kept coming to China over the centuries, and pilgrims travelled in the reverse direction to visit the holy places. This had the effect of preserving the Sanskrit and translated scriptures, in theory at least, close to their originals. A vast amount of scripture and commentary was compiled, however, and it is estimated that the Chinese Buddhist scriptures are over 700 times the size of the Bible.

In China the Buddha is always referred to under his clan name of Sakyamuni (or Shigiamuni). And the term Buddha is often used for the whole group of Bodhisattvas.

The new religion only won its way slowly in China. Some of its doctrines, notably that of rebirth, were foreign to China. The superiority of the Buddha to Confucius was challenged. On the other hand there were affinities between Buddhism and Taoism. The Buddhist belief in Nirvana was interpreted in the Taoist term "non-action" (*wu wei*). Other Taoist terms were used in translating the Buddhist scriptures, and on their side the Buddhists sometimes admitted Taoist deities into their temples.

The Indian Buddhist monks, Hinayana and Mahayana, by giving up their entire lives to residence in China, and being free from any form of political imperialism, gradually got their religion to take root. Not until A.D. 335 were Chinese allowed to become monks, but in times of public interest the monastic life was attractive and eventually large numbers became monks. This caused persecution from time to time.

Confucians had opposed Buddhism as foreign and unfilial, but the worst persecution came in 845 from a Taoist emperor of the Tang dynasty. His edict declared that there had been no Buddhism or Image-teaching in ancient China, but now they were "plundering the people's purse by golden decorations; ignoring parents and the sovereign in contributions; neglecting both husband and wife by their vigil-keeping; no teaching is more harmful than this Buddhism." Over 4,000 monasteries and 40,000 temples and meeting-places were confiscated or destroyed, and some 260,000 monks and nuns were ordered to return to secular life and pay taxes. If these figures are exaggerated, they show something of the strength of Buddhism by this time.

Yet despite this, and later, persecution Buddhism continued to grow. Although it had to contend with a highly developed philosophy, it attracted men of the keenest intellect and the highest social standing. It had a remarkable influence on art, poetry, and, later, the novel.

One sign of the vitality of Buddhism is seen in the rise of sects. Many of these came from India, but put on Chinese dress. The Wei Shih school of Pure Idealism had a great influence on the Confucians. Chan, a sect teaching meditation, arose in China and received considerable Taoist influence. It had a great effect on poetry and art. Later it spread to Japan where, as Zen, it is perhaps best known.

The "Pure Land" sect has been called the Bhakti (devotion) form of Mahayana Buddhism. It spread right across China, and into Korea and Japan. The founder was Hui Yuan (333–416), who had been a Taoist monk. The Taoist hope of a Western Paradise or Pure Land is taken as the goal of bliss, and it was largely through this conception that Buddhism gained a strong hold on the people. Amitabha Buddha is presented as the Merciful Father of the Ten Heavenly Regions, and faith in him is sufficient to gain an entrance into the Western Paradise.

The praise of Amitabha is declared in poems such as the Song of the White Lotus of the Pure Land in the West:

"No country is found so blissfully happy
As this land of purity far to the west.
There stands Amitabha in shining apparel . . .
Yes, God is the one, and on his throne seated,
He sends out his law to loose from all pain;
With arm gold-encircled, and crowned with jewels
He sends forth his power over sin, tears, and death."[1]

Salvation is by faith in Amitabha, by Bhakti love of the deity, rather than by works (*karma*). It is enough to call upon him. A popular verse says, "Whoever recites the name of Amitabha Buddha, whether in the present time or in future time, will surely see Amitabha Buddha and never become separated from him. He will become enlightened without resort to any other expedient means." The prayer, "I flee to thee Amitabha, Glory be to Amitabha," is uttered constantly and thousands of times a day by laity and monks in China and Japan. This short invocation of the sacred name has been called the Lord's Prayer of the Mahayana Buddhists. Amulets are worn bearing Amitabha's name, and pictures are made of him guiding the Ship of Salvation over the Sea of Sorrows to the haven of Paradise.

Side by side with Amitabha stands Kwanyin the "Goddess of Mercy". Women especially call upon her for the gift of children, and address her as "the Virgin who gives offspring". Innumerable prayers are offered to her also for entry into the Western Paradise.

[1] K. L. Reichelt, *Religion in Chinese Garment*, pp. 125–6.

There are many other divinities in the Buddhist pantheon. As Buddhas they are higher than the gods, since they have got beyond the causal chain of *karma*. Their images, many of them works of great art, are innumerable. Sakyamuni sits on a lotus vase with his eyes half-closed in meditation. Sometimes he is depicted as sleeping on his side, entering into Nirvana; or occasionally he appears as a little child. A popular figure is Maitreya, the Buddha to come, who holds a bag containing the future's gifts of fortune. Many other figures are found: some are versions of Indian gods such as Brahma and Indra, others are local deities and Chinese figures like Confucius.

It may well be thought that in adopting such an infinite pantheon Mahayana Buddhism has turned far away from the teaching of Gotama, and from the developments of Hinayana lands. But monks and teachers defend the worship of Amitabha and other divinities as uniting all the Buddhas and setting one on the road to perfection. Passing through levels of development and various paradises, one is led to absorption in Buddha and the utter peace of Nirvana where all desire and rebirth have ceased. Even in the Pure Land doctrine, salvation only became possible through Amitabha's first attaining supreme enlightenment, and those who find it difficult to reach enlightenment themselves in this world are assured of getting it in their next life by being born into Amitabha's land.

BUDDHIST WORSHIP

Buddhist buildings in China consist of monasteries, temples, and pagodas. The monasteries were quite comfortable, with cells containing raised beds, books, stools, and a table, and usually a statue of Amitabha. Few monks kept up the round with the begging-bowl that still obtains in Hinayana countries, and the Chinese monks had three meals a day, vegetarian but quite adequate. There are normally three services a day, at which bells are struck and formulas chanted, and rice and tea are placed on the altar. In many places incense burns day and night. Meditation is much less regular than in Burma. Strange though it may appear, the ancestral tablets have been cared for and offerings and prayers made for the dead in the Confucian way.

The monasteries may contain temples, and there are also local public temples, often originally used for some god who had no connection with Buddhism. Many of them were situated in delightful country, by rivers or on mountain tops. Trees are planted round about, and pools are found covered with lotuses, the flowers of purity. In our day, many monasteries and temples have been taken over for use as schools and public meeting-places.

The many-storeyed pagodas are well-known as typical of the Chinese scene. They are not temples, but originally covered relics of saints. Now they may be used for the purpose of "wind-and-water", and for divination. To-day many of them are falling into ruin.

We have already mentioned the part played by Buddhism in funeral and ancestral ceremonies. By their prayers or "masses" for the dead the monks have taken a vital part in public life. From the temples the sound of bells indicates that monks are telling the beads of their rosaries for the benefit of the souls in Hades. In the towns great processions have been held towards helping the departed. Memorials of those drowned in rivers take the form of lighting paper boats which are launched on the stream. A great deal of money has been spent on candles, incense, and paper objects to assist the dead, so much so that the rich were impoverished and the poor sunk in debt. Pilgrimages also have long been made under the auspices of Buddhism to sacred mountains, to pray that sickness might be cured or misfortune averted.

The introduction of prayers for the departed, which began in the seventh century, did much to recommend Buddhism to the Chinese who paid such attention to the cult of the ancestors. The tolerance and universalism of Buddhism, and its lack of a controlling doctrinal authority, helped it to adopt practices and beliefs that were foreign to its origin but which integrated it into the religious complex of China.

Both Islam and Christianity have a long history in China, but neither has yet succeeded in becoming part of general Chinese religious life, no doubt largely because of the strict demands of these monotheistic religions.

There are said to be anything between ten and twenty million Muslims in China, but they are mostly in the north-western provinces. Far away though China is from Arabia, the progress of the Arab armies was already felt in the late seventh century A.D. In 713 an Arab embassy visited the Chinese imperial court. Arab troops helped to quell a Tartar rebellion in 755, and were allowed to settle in China and marry Chinese women, but the men kept to their own religion.

Later Muslim immigrants brought Arab astronomical and mathematical knowledge, and some were employed by the Mongol rulers, Jenghiz Khan and Kublai Khan. In the eighteenth century there was a Muslim rebellion, which was followed by such repressive laws against them that in 1863 they rose again and there was terrible slaughter of hundreds of thousands of people on both sides. This fighting greatly weakened the Muslims, and made them hated by others.

The Muslims have never fully mixed with non-Muslims, and they have not done much to spread their religion in China, being content with their own mosques and schools. Their mosques are generally like other Chinese temples, without minarets. Of course there are no images. The faithful turn to the west, towards Mecca, when praying. Some Muslims take part in village idol-festivals, and many neglect circumcision. The women are not veiled. There are pilgrimages to Mecca, but visitors from Arabia look on Chinese Islam as corrupt. Arabic is used in reading the Quran but few understand it. At Canton there is a tomb supposed to be that of Muhammad's uncle, and many pilgrims visit it.

Christianity also seems to have arrived in China by the seventh century, brought by the strongly missionary church of the Nestorians, who believed in the existence of two distinct divine and human persons in Christ. Inscriptions are still to be discovered which tell of this church, and recent finds include pictures of crosses and of angels with mandarin-like beards.

One of these inscriptions gives an interesting text which shows the adaptation of Christian teaching. "The brilliant and reverend Mi-shih-he [Messiah], veiling and hiding his true majesty, came to earth in the likeness of man. An angel proclaimed the good news; a virgin gave birth to the sage. . . . He hung up a brilliant sun to take by storm the halls of darkness; the wiles of the devil were then all destroyed. He rowed the boat of mercy to go up to the palace of light; those who have souls were then completely saved. His mighty works thus finished, he ascended at midday to the spiritual sphere."[1]

The Nestorian Christians seem to have been badly hit by a Taoist persecution in the ninth century. When Franciscan monks came to China in the thirteenth and fourteenth centuries, they found some of the old Christians' descendants still in existence. The Franciscan missions failed when foreigners were expelled in the fourteenth century; they had not succeeded in establishing a Chinese priesthood. Then the Jesuits came (fifteenth–sixteenth centuries). They sought to gain the ears of scholars, and adopted mandarin dress and studied the classics. By their knowledge they made themselves useful to the imperial court at Peking. They spread to many parts of China, training Chinese priests. Like the Buddhists, the Jesuits found that the Chinese people loved ornate services and decorations and became devoted to "Jesus the Master of Heaven" and the "Holy Mother".

The Jesuits had allowed their converts to continue to pay their reverence to the ancestors. Later Franciscan and Dominican missionaries were not so accommodating, and after bitter controversy the emperor intervened and only allowed those missionaries to remain who permitted the Confucian rites for the dead. Meantime the Pope had forbidden all missionaries to allow these. This check, and later slackening of effort, greatly reduced the numbers of Christians.

[1] A. C. Moule, *Christians in China before the Year 1550*, pp. 34ff.

In the nineteenth century Protestant missionaries arrived and did a great deal for the education of China in western ways of thought, and also for the translation of the Chinese classics. Unfortunately their cause was prejudiced by the colonial and commercial activities of other Europeans, and Christianity was associated with foreign ways. Nevertheless the churches not only did great work in education and medicine, but also Chinese priests and bishops were trained. There were 7,000 Protestant missionaries in China in 1930. After the Communist revolution and victory in 1949 both Protestant and Roman Catholic missionaries were expelled and soon hardly one remained. It remains to be seen how far the modern Chinese Church has become indigenous and able to stand up to the strains of modern life. It has been reckoned to amount to not more than one per cent of the population, but its influence on thought has been out of all proportion to its numbers.

RELIGION IN CHINA TO-DAY

We have treated briefly of religious life in the past, under the heading of the three religions and ancestor-worship. It remains to say a word about the chances of religious life to-day.

How are the old religious beliefs and practices of China standing up to life under a Communist regime? It is not easy to obtain adequate information, but certain currents of opinion can be observed.

Confucianism has suffered a series of blows in this century. The first was the abolition of the examinations in the classics in 1907. Then with the fall of the Manchu dynasty in 1911 the ceremonies of the Imperial Sacrifices were abolished, and the sole attempt made by the first president to continue the ritual only helped to bring about his fall. There have been efforts towards a neo-Confucian revival and introduction of its morality into schools, but this has been changed again with the coming of the Communists to power. An expensive project to rebuild and glorify the temple at Confucius' birthplace was dropped during the Sino-Japanese war.

Many of the leading Communists are outspokenly hostile to

the Chinese classical system. Mao Tse-Tung has said, "I hated Confucius from the age of eight."[1] The chief criticism of Confucianism is that it is feudal and reactionary, and that its entire tradition has been closely associated with the past "feudal ruling class". Millions of young Chinese, who formerly would have studied Confucius and the classics, now spend hours every day reading the works of Marx, Lenin, Stalin, and Mao Tse-tung. Moreover, family life has been disrupted, women have been given a larger place in affairs, and children have been taught to denounce their parents as reactionaries.

Yet repairs to the temple of heaven at Peking, and the issue of the state calendar which formerly was the prerogative of the emperor, suggest that modern Chinese are not wholly blind to the importance of state religion. And it seems difficult to think that China, having thrown off what is foreign, will continue to renounce its own peculiar heritage. The new ruling class may well find it expedient to adopt the old Confucian injunctions to obedience in due time.

Some of the classics, notably the Classic of Poetry, have been re-issued in modern form. The theatre has been used for propaganda, with old plays rewritten. Modern scholarship shows that Confucius was a reformer and a friend of the poor, and that his pride and "feudal" teaching are inventions of the later ruling classes who perverted his teaching for their own uses. Sun Yat-sen, the republican president, recognized this truth and declared that "both Confucius and Mencius were exponents of democracy". At least one leading Communist has recently supported this view.

The popular religious beliefs remain, some of them changing, others reappearing in new guise. China is predominantly an agricultural country and many ancient rituals have survived. Changes come more slowly in the villages and among the women. It is the mothers and grandmothers who keep up the old customs, burning incense daily before the family shrines and making pilgrimages to the mountains.

The future of Taoism is debated. It has come under attack

[1] H. G. Creel, *Chinese Thought, from Confucius to Mao Tse-tung*, p. 265.

for its superstitions and mercenary practices. Many Buddhist and Taoist monasteries and temples and their lands have been expropriated for common use. The monks have been told to give up the life of parasitic drones and take up useful occupations. Taoism lacks organization and leadership. Some writers regard it as moribund. But others consider Taoism to have a more fundamental hold than Buddhism on the Chinese people. Taoism is truly Chinese. It has been said that in the struggle of Communism to root out religion, Taoism may prove the toughest opponent, very much like the Chinese dragon which cannot be grasped by its head or its tail.

The loss of its buildings and lands should not be fatal to Buddhism, for in the origins of this religion Gotama taught the life of poverty. Nevertheless Buddhism has depended mainly upon its monks, who have been its true church, and it remains to be seen how they can subsist in the modern world. The Communists have recognized that Buddhism has the largest following of any religion among the common people of China. Buddhism has survived bitter persecutions in the past, with the destruction of its monasteries and dispersal of its monks, and it may well weather the present storm.

Although strong among the people, and once very influential among the educated, Buddhism has not been so important in intellectual circles in China in recent centuries. But there are some signs of revival and reform. There are great resources in the morality and the scriptures of Buddhism, and it may be able to reform itself and gather new strength. Such reformation had already begun before the revolution, owing to the impact on Buddhism of Western education and Christianity.

NOTE ON LAMAISM

A peculiar form of Buddhism called Lamaism has flourished especially in Tibet. Lamaism is also found in Mongolia and has a considerable following in China, especially in the north and north-west. The Chinese Communist party has recently given huge sums for the renovation of the great Lama temple in Peking. Tibetan Lamaism is famous despite the inaccessibility of this mountainous and snowy country. The splendid buildings, the highly developed monastic institutions, and the complex rituals of Lamaism, which seem to resemble Roman Catholicism, are striking and interesting. Since we have said something of Mahayana Buddhism in China this seems the place to write briefly about its Lamaist forms.

The peculiar features of Tibetan Buddhism are not just of local manufacture, but owe a great deal to India. In some ways this is a form of degenerate Buddhism that obtained at a late date in parts of India, and such as is still found in Nepal. Tibetan art seems to have been founded on that of Nepal, but later in turn it imposed new forms on Nepalese art. One must not underestimate the Tibetan native contribution to its Buddhism. The Tibetans accepted a foreign faith, and translated many Sanskrit scriptures, but they evolved their church discipline to an extent never known in India. And they exaggerated the demonic element in Indian religion into grotesque and horrific forms.

Buddhism is said to have come to Tibet relatively late, in the seventh century A.D., hence long after its establishment in China. From then on monks came to Tibet over the centuries, and Lamaism (from Tibetan *blama*, a superior monk) is said to have been firmly established in the eighth century. There was a revival of the ancient animistic Bon religion of Tibet in the tenth century, and harsh persecution of Buddhism, but the latter was re-established in the following century. By the time of the Mongol empire in China Lamaism had become so powerful and well-known that Kublai Khan summoned a leading Lamaist to China and was himself initiated into the religion.

Tibet has been a theocracy, governed by priests. About one quarter of the country is composed of monks, who live in huge monasteries as complete communities. The head is the Dalai Lama, who is regarded as the incarnation of the Bodhisattva Avalokiteśvara. He has been called the "Pope" of Lamaism. When he dies he is thought to be reincarnated at once and search is made for a child who bears the sign of being the "living Buddha". The present Dalai Lama, the fourteenth, was chosen in 1933 when he was a boy of thirteen, and installed in 1939. He lives in the Potala, the great monastery of Lhasa.

There is a very large body of Tibetan scriptures, surprising for such a harsh country. But not only was Tibetan Buddhism in close touch with India, but also the size and extent of the monasteries helped the development of the scriptures.

In Tibetan belief and imagery Sakyamuni is the principal figure, and associated with him are previous Buddhas, and Maitreya, the Buddha to come. Amitabha and the Indian deities Sakya and Manjuśri are important. Great prominence is given to goddesses of whom the chief is Tara, described as the wife of Avalokiteśvara, and appearing now in benevolent and now in terrible shapes (like Kali the spouse of Śiva in India).

In religious practices we must notice the praying-wheels and prayer-flags. Such are also found in China and Japan, but not in India (except Nepal), and they seem to be a Tibetan invention. The wheel is a small barrel containing written prayers or books, and turned by hand or by the winds and streams. People carry small wheels in their hands. By the turning of the wheel people acquire all the merit that would come from reading the prayers or books, and this helps the journey to the Paradise of Amitabha.

Constant repetition is made of the formula *Om Mani Padme Hum*, revolved in the wheels, written on flags and rocks, and uttered by every human voice. The word *Om* is a mystic syllable derived from the Indian Upanishads, and *Hum* probably comes from the same word. *Mani Padme* is said to mean the jewel in the lotus, but its origin is obscure. It may be one of the names of Avalokiteśvara (Padmapani).

The two main sects of Tibet, distinguished by their hats, the Yellow Hats and the Red Hats, have different deities and scriptures, but these concern the monks rather than the people whose beliefs contain a good deal of primitive animism. The Yellow Hats (Gelugpa, "virtuous sect") always include the two leading figures of the state. These are the Dalai Lama and the Panchen Lama, the latter regarded as an incarnation of Amitabha.

When the Chinese Communists invaded Tibet in 1950, the Panchen Lama was first proclaimed as rightful ruler of Tibet. He had been educated in China and was proclaimed in Peking. The Red Hats who are strong in eastern Tibet also hoped to seize power. The Dalai Lama at first fled before the Chinese advance, each place that he stayed at in his flight to Nepal becoming a holy shrine as the abode of "the living Buddha". But the Chinese soon found that they could not impose a ruler on the Tibetans who had only limited authority and was not recognized as the rightful ruler. They invited the Dalai Lama to return, which he did and went to Peking to negotiate a settlement.

An agreement was signed which respected Tibet's autonomy, and guaranteed religious freedom and the maintenance of Tibetan habits and customs. Only military and foreign affairs were to be under Chinese direction. How far this may eventually affect monastic and religious life cannot be said.

Short Bibliography

E. R. and K. Hughes, *Religion in China* (Hutchinson)
B. S. Bonsall, *Confucianism and Taoism* (Epworth)
C. H. S. Ward, *Buddhism, Vol. 2. Mahayana* (Epworth)
Liu Wu-Chi, *A Short History of Confucian Philosophy* (Pelican)
W. E. Soothill, *The Analects of Confucius* (World's Classics)
E. R. Hughes, *Chinese Philosophy in Classical Times* (Everyman)
L. Giles, *The Book of Mencius* (Murray)
——, *The Sayings of Lao-Tzu* (Murray)
——, *Taoist Teachings* (Murray)
A. Waley, *The Way and the Power* (Allen & Unwin)
J. E. Ellam, *The Religion of Tibet* (Murray)
A. David-Neel, *With Mystics and Magicians in Tibet* (Penguin)
S. Kaizuka, *Confucius* (Allen & Unwin)
Lin Yutang, *The Wisdom of China* (Joseph)

6

Japanese Religion

In Japan a national religion, Shinto, "the Way of the Gods", survives from prehistoric times. Buddhism and Confucianism came late, but Buddhism in particular naturalized itself in Japan by identifying itself with learning and ethics. Whereas in China Buddhism had had to contend with a highly developed native philosophy and culture, in Japan it brought great cultural changes and exercised a powerful influence over religion and education.

Ancient inhabitants of the Japanese islands in the New Stone Age left behind them traces of stone, shell, and pottery. If their religion was like that of the present aboriginal peoples (Ainus) of the northern island then they worshipped the sun, the spirit of fire which is still revered at every pagan hearth, and the still sacred mountain Fujiyama. Demons were feared and exorcism practised.

About the beginning of the Christian era invaders entered Japan from Korea. They were at the Iron Age level, and not only have iron axes and swords been found but bits and stirrups which show that horses were used. In tombs that they have left, great stones covered with earthen mounds, iron objects are present and also terra cotta figures which may represent human beings buried with the dead. The religion of these ancestors of the Japanese is seen partly in archaeological remains and partly in the myths of early Shinto.

SHINTO

The word Shinto is derived from Chinese and means "the Way of the Gods" or spirits (*Shen Tao*). It was not used until the introduction of Buddhism and Chinese culture to Japan in the sixth century A.D. made it necessary to distinguish the new religion from the old national way. The Japanese pronunciation of the same characters is *Kami no Michi*.

The word used for Gods, Kami, means "above" or "superior". It can be used of powers that are revered or feared, heaven and earth, seas, mountains, trees, uncanny animals, and special human beings like emperors. One leading authority says, "There are many cases of seas and mountains being called Kami. It is not their spirits which are meant. The word was applied directly to the seas and mountains themselves, as being very awful things."

Writing came late to Japan, being introduced from China in the fifth to sixth centuries A.D. Under the impact of Chinese and Buddhist scriptures, the Shinto sacred myths were recorded in the eighth century. The best of the early documents of Shinto myths are "Chronicles" called Kojiki and Nihongi. Prayers and rituals were written down later, from the eighth to the tenth centuries; the Yengi Shiki and the Manyo-Shiu contain many prayers and poems. But behind these documents are centuries of memorized tradition.

The myths of Shinto are many and fantastic, charming and often crude, and with little moral teaching. There is a creation myth of the universe as a sea of mud shrouded in darkness. Several gods appear and disappear, separating heaven and earth. Then a divine couple, "The Male-who-Invites" and "The Female-who-Invites" (Izanagi and Izanami), begat the Japanese islands and spirits of mountains, winds, food, and fire. Finally from them came gods that have become famous: the Sun-goddess (Amaterasu, the Heaven-Illumining Goddess), the Moon-god (Tsuki-yomi), and the Storm-god (Susanowo, Valiant-Swift-Impetuous-Hero).

Amaterasu, the Sun-goddess, then shared the rule of the universe with her brother the Storm-god, Susanowo. He behaved badly to her and she took refuge in the Cave of Heaven and left the world in darkness. She was only enticed out by a dance organized by all the other gods. A mirror had been hung outside her cave, and when she peeped out she

117

saw her own reflection and advanced to examine it, whereupon another god seized her hand and pulled her out. Susanowo was then tried by the gods and banished to Izumo, on the northern coast of Japan, and finally to the Nether Land.

This fanciful story is a sun-myth, explaining the retirement of the sun in eclipse, storm, and winter, and the banishment of storm and darkness to the world below. Amaterasu has become the most important Shinto deity, and some have called her the Supreme Being. But this is hardly correct, since celestial affairs were settled by a council of gods. Amaterasu has the greatest Shinto shrine in Japan, at Ise on the south coast, where her mirror (sun-form-mirror) is kept in a box and treated with the greatest reverence. The second greatest shrine is that of Izumo where Susanowo, and especially his son the Earth-god, Ohonamochi, are worshipped.

A further important myth tells how Amaterasu dispossessed Ohonamochi from ruling over the earth, and gave the rule of all Japan to her grandson Ninigi. Ninigi came down from heaven and married the goddess of Mount Fuji. One of their great-grandchildren was claimed as the first Emperor of Japan, Jimmu Tenno. He is said by tradition to have lived in 660 B.C., but modern scholars put his date about 40 B.C. The emperor was thus believed to be of divine descent, and this provided justification for the State Shinto cult whose traditions were taught in all schools in Japan before the war. Three Sacred Imperial Treasures, mirror, jewels, and sword, were held to be of divine origin. The mirror is kept at Ise, the sword at another shrine, and the jewels in the royal palace at Tokyo. Reference will be made later to modern forms of State Shinto.

Many other gods are worshipped in the popular Shinto cults. After the Sun-goddess the most important is the "Food-possessor" (Uke-mochi), the spirit of food and sometimes of drink. A variant of this goddess is the Rice-god (Inari), who has shrines in every village. The fox is his messenger and is often regarded as the god himself.

The shrines of the gods are small and simple, and very numerous. They are made of wood and have thatched or wooden roofs. They are rebuilt every twenty years, but always on traditional patterns. These are small dwellings for the gods and are not usually open to the public. Priests perform the ceremonies and ritual dances. There are symbols, such as mirror and sword, but no ancient images since images only came in with Buddhism. At the entrance to the shrine is a typical wooden gateway, or several arches, and ropes mark off the most sacred areas. Symbols of sanctity are the *gohei*, small poles in which are inserted pieces of paper or cloth. Groves of tall and ancient trees, which are always to be found at the shrines, give an atmosphere of age and silence and express the Japanese love of nature. At Ise there are great sacred areas, the inner shrine being over three miles away from the outer shrine.

Shinto is far from being a "primitive" cult. There is an organized priesthood and an elaborate ritual. There are public rituals at the ancient state shrines. There are also family and village gods which have their festivals. It is essentially a religion of gratitude and love. The festivals are of a joyous character, and the gods are addressed as parents and divine ancestors.

There is conflicting opinion among scholars as to whether ancestor worship was part of primitive Shinto. It seems to have come over from China. Shinto had no doctrine of the immortality of the soul and seems to have avoided funeral ceremonies. But under the influence of Buddhism prayers to the dead came in. In the homes of the people there are small shelves bearing shrines to the family ancestors to which daily offerings are made.

The moral teaching of early Shinto was very elementary. There were recognized social crimes, but little teaching about them in the sacred books. There were rituals for purification from defilement, but there was a very limited sense of sin. In later sects there is more emphasis on purity of heart.

THE BUDDHIST NATURALIZATION

Buddhism first came to Japan from Korea in the sixth century A.D. Korea itself had received Buddhism, together with Chinese writing, in the fourth century. Korean Buddhism differs little from that of China and Japan, but it has been handicapped by the monks taking part in politics and even fighting in war. Korea was the medium for transmitting Chinese writing and Buddhism to Japan, and at first Korean monks played an important part in Japanese religion and art. But as soon as they were able to do so the Japanese by-passed Korea and went straight to China.

The first mission from a Korean king to the Japanese emperor with the Buddhist message included images and books. The message said, "This religion is the most excellent of all teachings. . . . It brings endless and immeasurable blessings and fruits to its believers, even the attainment of supreme enlightenment (*bodhi*). . . . Moreover, the religion has come over to Korea far from India, and the peoples are now ardent followers of its teaching, and none are outside its pale."[1]

After some early setbacks Buddhism was greatly strengthened by the accession of the Prince-Regent Shotoku, in 593. He proclaimed Buddhism as the religion of the state and established a grand Buddhist institution, with temples, asylum, hospital, and dispensary. The Prince gave lectures on Buddhist scriptures, notably the "Lotus of the Wonderful Law" which interprets the life of Buddha Sakyamuni as a manifestation of eternal truth and a gospel of universal salvation. The Prince thought of himself as a Bodhisattva, and later generations saw in him an incarnation of Kwannon, the Lord of Mercy (the Chinese Kwanyin, Goddess of Mercy).

In the eighth century the emperor Shomu ordered images of the Buddha to be erected in the provinces, along with dispensaries and other public works. He built a great temple at his capital of Nara, with a colossal bronze figure of the Buddha, said to be the largest bronze in the world. It is "a bronze statue more than fifty feet in height, seated on a gigantic lotus pedestal. The enormous halo is studded with minor statues of Buddhas and saints, while on the pedestal are engraved scenes of the twenty-five realms of existence

[1] M. Anesaki, *History of Japanese Religion*, p. 53.

with the figures of celestial and terrestrial beings—all united in adoration of the central figures and glorifying the majesty of the Supremely Enlightened."[1]

Buddhism succeeded in taking root in Japan because of its all-embracing nature, and it took Shinto to itself. At Nara, Shinto shrines still adjoin Buddhist temples. When he was about to build the temple at Nara, the emperor Shomu sent a Buddhist priest to the shrine of the Sun-goddess at Ise with a present of a Buddhist relic. The priest brought back a message that the Sun-goddess identified herself with Vairocana, one of the Bodhisattvas of the Mahayana school (perhaps himself originally a sun-god). However successful was this identifying of Shinto and Buddhist deities, it helped to hide the figure of Gotama the Buddha behind the sun-gods.

The whole pantheon of Shinto gods were regarded as manifestations of Vairocana. This was systematized in the teaching of a popular sect called Ryobu Shinto, "the twofold way of the gods". Buddhism took the upper hand, by its higher ideals, and for long Shinto deities were only vaguely recognized. Buddhist priests took charge of most of the Shinto shrines, except such important ones as Ise and Izumo. Many Buddhist images were introduced. Most of the emperors, who were high priests of Shinto, took the Buddhist monk's tonsure.

For a thousand years Buddhism triumphed, until the great Shinto reaction in the nineteenth century. Before we come to this, it is well at this point to mention some of the Buddhist sects which have been so important in Japan, though not all are still alive.

BUDDHIST SECTS

It is common to speak of twelve Buddhist sects in Japan, but only the most important are mentioned here.

The Tendai sect came from China in the Nara period and because of its all-embracing character, allowing for many ways of approaching the truth, it was able to help in the unification of the empire. The sect emphasizes the *unity* of

[1] Op. cit., p. 89.

everything in Buddha's love. Its extreme tolerance of all forms tends to allow the distinctive Buddhist teaching to be covered over with a mass of other material. The Shingon sect is similarly comprehensive; it is a low form of Indian Buddhism giving much place to mystical ritual and incantation.

The Jodo sect is the Japanese name for the popular Chinese "Pure Land" sect. It is a revolt against formalism and dogma, and has been likened to the Lutheran stress on salvation by faith alone. The believer turns in pure faith to Amida (Amitabha), the Buddha of Infinite Light and Lord of the Western Paradise. Amida had acquired enough merit to save all who call upon him in the formula "Adoration to the Buddha of Infinite Light". By reciting the name of Amida, or even calling on him once in the hour of death, a man can be saved. A development of Jodo was the Jodo-Shin sect which taught such absolute reliance on faith that celibacy and monasticism were rejected, and even priests may marry and eat meat.

Against this arose the Nichiren sect in the thirteenth century, denouncing Jodo as deceit and blasphemy. Nichiren denounced the worship of Amida, Vairocana, and the Bodhisattvas, and called men back to the one eternal Buddha, Sakyamuni. However, this was not a recall to the Gotama of history, but to the exalted Sakyamuni of the Lotus scripture.

"In Nichiren's bosom, in his body of the flesh, is secretly enshrined the great mystery which the Lord Sakyamuni transmitted to me on the Vulture Peak. Therefore it is that in my breast all Buddhas are immersed in contemplation, on my tongue they turn the wheel of the Law, in my throat they are born, and in my mouth they attain enlightenment."[1]

Thus convinced of the truth of his own message, and the falsehood of others, Nichiren persecuted other sects and was exiled himself. There are more Jodo than Nichiren followers to-day.

Perhaps the most interesting Japanese Buddhist sect, and a most lively one to-day, is Zen. The name Zen is derived from the Chinese Chan and Pali Dhyana, and means a technique of

[1] Quoted by Eliot, *Japanese Buddhism*, p. 430.

meditation; but Zen has flowered in Japan much more than in the western lands whence it came. Zen rejects the intellectual and philosophical solutions to the problems of life, and teaches that knowledge comes by a sudden enlightenment. Thus it is an experience, rather than a doctrine. It is an intuition, whereby men see their relationship to the Buddha-nature. Enlightenment comes not by striving, but by realization of the spiritual reality all around. The Chinese Zen masters had related the enlightenment to the "vision of the Tao". It is an illumination which comes "like the bottom of a tub falling out".

Despite the stress on sudden enlightenment, the Zen monks and disciples undergo strict training in *za-zen*, a kind of meditation, and perform manual labour. Also they are the only Japanese sect which continues the daily begging-round prescribed by the Buddha. Strangely enough, Zen became the creed of the military class in Japan and gave direction to the Bushido, or code of chivalry. This is due to the discipline taught by Zen and suppression of self-interest, which recommended it to the knights (Samurai). Both archery and the wrestling sport of Ju-jutsu were taken up as part of the technique of self-mastery. Warriors hid small Buddhist images in their hair, or a prayer leaflet underneath their armour. But while Zen helped to humanize war, its knightly followers abandoned the peaceful foundation of Buddhism.

Zen meditation is described in terms not unlike the Indian Yoga. "The devotee takes up his position with his legs crossed and the soles of his feet uppermost (the lotus posture). His back is held straight, but not rigidly, the palm of his right hand facing upwards and its back contained in the palm of the left hand which rests, knuckles downwards, on his lap. His eyes are kept half-closed, his mouth is slightly open and the tip of his tongue rests lightly at the base of his upper teeth. This position can be maintained for hours by those who have had sufficient experience, and there are even some who can maintain it for days. After taking up this posture the seeker after Enlightenment allows a few moments for his thoughts to become calm, and then strives to put his mind into a condition to receive the intuitive knowledge which, it is believed, enters only when the mind is perfectly still and devoid of thoughts. . . . The degrees of success range from the ability to keep the mind tranquil for a few moments to ecstatic contemplation lasting over a long period and leading to supreme Enlightenment."[1]

Monks of all sects repeat daily the threefold refuge, in Buddha, Law and Order,. and the Mahayanist vows, "However innumerable beings are, I vow to save them; however inexhaustible the passions are I vow to extinguish them." All the Amidist sects utter the prayer to Amida called the Nembutsu (from Namu Amida Butsu), "Adoration to Amida Buddha".

All the Buddhist sects, including Zen and Nichiren, constantly use the Kwannon Sutra, from the "Lotus of the Wonderful Law" which has been called "the New Testament of Japan". These are a few extracts from the Kwannon chapter:

"World-honoured One, for what reason is Kwanzeon Bosatsu [Kwannon Bodhisattva] so named? The Buddha said . . . 'Even when people fall into a great fire, if they hold the name of Kwanzeon Bosatsu, the fire will not scorch them because of the spiritual power of this Bosatsu. . . . When hundreds of thousands of people go out into the great ocean . . . their boats may be wrecked by black storms . . . if among them there is even a single person who will utter the name of Kwanzeon Bosatsu all the people will be released from the disaster. . . .

If a woman desire a male child, let her worship and make offerings to Kwanzeon Bosatsu, and she will have a male child fully endowed with bliss and wisdom. If she desire a female child, she will have one graceful in features. . . .

If there are beings in any country who are to be saved by his assuming a Buddha-form, Kwanzeon Bosatsu will manifest himself in the form of a Buddha and will preach to them the Dharma.'"[2]

[1] J. Blofeld, The Jewel in the Lotus, p. 136.
[2] D. T. Suzuki, Manual of Zen Buddhism, pp. 30-3.

There was no official introduction of Confucianism in Japan, as there was of Buddhism. During the seventh and eighth centuries, in the glory of the Tang dynasty in China, when everything Chinese was being copied in Japan, and the Tang culture was being transferred almost bodily to the Japanese Imperial Court, then Confucianism came in also. As one Japanese writer says, "In the midst of the sea of importations Confucianism sailed in, not so much for its ethics and metaphysics as because it was the guiding principle of the political and social institutions" of China.

It was particularly in its stress on filial duty and piety, and attention to the ancestors, that Confucianism filled a lack in Japanese life. The Chinese habit of placarding the names of those distinguished for dutifulness to their parents, was adopted in Japan; while those who had committed the sin of filial disobedience were sent away in disgrace to distant provinces. Even devoted Buddhist emperors ordered the close study of the Confucian classic, "The doctrine of Filial Dutifulness".

However, it seems that Confucianism did little to affect the morality of the common people or to deliver them from their superstitions. The Chinese method of divination, in the interaction of Yin and Yang, the female and male principles, was practised under the name of Confucius.

Several schools of Confucianism arose in Japan. In them were expressed the tensions inherent in Confucianism between the ethical on the one hand and the religious or philosophical on the other. Confucius himself had been eminently practical and had refused to speculate in religious matters, yet he seems to have had an ingrained belief in Heaven and in his divine commission. Some of his Japanese followers taught the unity of the spirit of man and the reason of the universe. This leads to the brotherhood of man, "All things in the world come from one root, and so all men in the four seas who are, so to speak, its branches, must be brothers of one another." On the other hand, by becoming one with nature man tends to lose his personality. "At death man shall return to the all-pervading spirit, as a vapour in the sky melts away, as a drop mingles with the sea, as fire disappears in fire."

In the seventeenth century there was a reaction to practical Confucianism in Japan, with a return to the study of the classical books. The aim of Confucianism is benevolence and justice, and the development of the self so as to produce right conduct. The Confucian emphasis on loyalty had a strong influence on the Samurai or aristocratic class, and together with Zen Buddhism it helped to create the ideal of chivalry. But here Confucianism was transformed, the devoted soldier takes the place of the virtuous scholar as the ideal of the perfect man. The effect of this application of Confucianism to chivalry was to strengthen the movement for fanatical devotion to the state represented in the sacred person of the emperor.

STATE SHINTO

In 1549 St Francis Xavier had landed in Japan and the Christian message enjoyed a rapid success. Apparently this was partly because Christianity seemed to come from India (Xavier had met his Japanese guide at Goa), and partly because the feudal lord of Kyushu, the southern island of Japan where Xavier had landed, was glad to have foreign support in his struggles for power with other feudal lords. The self-sacrificing and ardent Christian missionaries contrasted favourably with the corrupt priesthood of Japan, even if the new faith was less accommodating towards idolatry than Buddhism had been. So many converts were made that, it is said, Xavier's hands were heavy with baptizing. Eventually over a million people are said to have been converted.

Christian missions, however, soon became suspect because of their association with foreign powers, the authority of the Pope and the vessels of the Portuguese traders. Their propaganda was first forbidden in 1587. The Jesuits worked cautiously, trying to interest influential families, but when more missionaries (Franciscans) arrived, persecution began. Twenty-six missionaries and converts were crucified, and this was the signal for a long series of martyrdoms. The coming of more missions, and English and Dutch traders, only aggravated the situation. Thousands of Christians died for their faith. Sometimes they rose in arms in desperation, and this made things worse so that there were huge massacres. By 1640 Christian influence was practically at an end. There remained hidden Christians, and their descendants were discovered by French priests when the country was reopened in 1868.

This opposition to Christianity and Europe brought an intensely anti-foreign spirit, which isolated Japan from the rest of the world for over two hundred years, under the rule of the Tokugawa Shoguns (dictators). As against foreign influences scholars were urged to undertake more intensive study of the pure and primitive Shinto as the national faith of Japan. Even Buddhism, after its thousand years of naturalization in Japan, was regarded as foreign.

In the eighteenth century an important theologian, Motoori, began a movement to purge Shinto of all foreign influences, especially Buddhist. He declared that Shinto represented the purest and best teaching of mankind, and he rejected the religious and ethical teachings which had come to Japan from abroad in Buddhism and Confucianism. Shinto was the only true religion, not only of Japan but of mankind, and hence the Japanese people and their emperor had a divine right to rule the whole world.

The myth of the descent of the royal line from the Sun-goddess, Amaterasu, was now brought to the forefront again. The submission of the Earth-god to her grandson Ninigi was taken as a model for the submission of all peoples to the emperor of Japan.

It may be said here that the statement often made that Shinto is emperor-worship needs qualification. Only a small number of past emperors have shrines, and most of these are recent innovations. The imperial ancestors have been worshipped collectively at a private shrine in the Hall of Imperial Spirits in the Palace at Tokyo. The twenty-odd public shrines of emperors can be added to, of course, and this practice, along with the recent cult of the war dead, became immensely popular in the nineteenth and twentieth centuries.

The work of Moto-ori was continued by Hirata, with violent attacks on Buddhism and Confucianism. For a time they had little popular following, owing to the great strength of Buddhism. But in the nineteenth century the western nations, especially Russia and America, came knocking at Japan's door. There was great agitation in Japan, summed up in slogans such as: "Adore the throne and expel the barbarians", and "Adore the throne and supplant the Shogun". In 1867 the Shogun (dictator) gave back his power and title, and the Emperor Meiji was brought out of his sacred seclusion to become the active ruler of a modern state. His capital was moved to Tokyo, and the former palace of the Shoguns became the Imperial Palace.

With the restoration of the Emperor (the Mikado), Shinto received a great impetus. The Dual Shinto (Ryobu Shinto), which had combined Shinto with Buddhism, was abolished. Buddhist images and books were banished from Shinto shrines. Shinto was proclaimed the religion of the Japanese state, and put under the care of the highest government department. All privileges of the Buddhist clergy were abolished and much property confiscated. The old Chinese science and Confucian ethics were denounced as stupid, and the Confucian teachers were called "rotten literati". The new education from America and Europe was hailed as the sole means of progress. Thus the new era saw at once a revival of Shinto and also a welcoming of Western culture.

At first Buddhism was badly shaken by this bitter attack. But being forced back on her own deep reserves Buddhism gradually gathered strength and returned to favour. It came to be realized in official circles that Buddhism was too deeply enrooted in the people's affections to be abolished. Buddhists infiltrated into the governmental ecclesiastical department, and in 1877 Buddhism was granted autonomy.

With the opening of Japan to the West, Christian missionaries had returned. Their converts and descendants of the old Catholics were arrested under the old law. But strong protest by foreign powers caused the withdrawal of the prohibition of Christianity. Christianity has now been recognized as a religion firmly rooted in Japan. Its modern adherents number about half a million.

The effect of recognizing Buddhism and Christianity as religions brought the same treatment to the old "shrine" Shinto, the ancient worship of the powers of nature. The communal State Shinto cult, and the ceremonies performed by the emperor, were regarded as civil rites and as having nothing to do with religion. From this it was an easy step to make the observance of State Shinto obligatory for everybody of Japanese citizenship, and for all subject races, whatever their religion might be.

State Shinto was said to be not a religion but a national obligation, with a prior claim over all religious allegiance. Christians and Buddhists were told to attend the state shrines as a sign of reverence to the Imperial Ancestors. There was little in practice, however, to distinguish the large State Shrines such as Ise from the smaller country shrines. State Shinto was also taught in all schools. Christians and Buddhists found their children being sent to any local Shinto shrine that happened to be handy, however superstitious the worship there.

Such was the position up to the end of the Second World War. The fanatical loyalty of Japanese was the product of the state cult of the Divine Emperor. With the defeat of the Japanese, the state gods seemed to have failed to save the nation. Nevertheless the emperor has survived as a constitutional ruler. The chief condition of surrender which the Japanese made early in 1945 was that the emperor should be allowed to remain. This was refused by the allies. But after the atomic bombs had been dropped on Hiroshima, Japan was brought to her knees and peace was made unconditionally. Despite this complete collapse, the emperor was allowed to remain, but in 1946 he broadcast a public repudiation of his divine ancestry.

The State Shinto shrines were disestablished, some three hundred of them, by the allied military leaders. The teaching of Shinto in the schools was forbidden. This has meant the desertion of many shrines and poverty for priests. The future of Shinto cannot be predicted.

Buddhism and Christianity are both making efforts to gain the religious leadership of the Japanese people. But many Japanese are turning away from Buddhism, feeling that it has little to say to the problems of the new Japan; there seems to be more enthusiasm for the Buddhist faith in some of the Pacific islands. Another potent religious influence is to be found in the Shinto sects, which we must consider briefly.

SECT SHINTO

The development of Sect Shinto is comparatively modern. As the sects have not been under state control they have been the more free to develop according to the religious needs of the people. They have their own teaching, organization, and "churches" for congregational worship.

Out of the eighty-five millions of Japan some seventeen millions are said to belong to the Shinto sects. Thirteen of these sects are officially recognized. Three of them are Pure Shinto, being opposed to the secular State Shinto, and seeking to interpret the traditional myths in ways that will make the religion popular. There are two Confucian sects, which teach Confucian ethics against a background of Shinto belief. Then there are sects which centre on the worship of gods of mountains such as Fujiyama.

The most interesting of the sects are the Faith-Healing variety, in which an approach to Christian ideas may be seen. The Konko-kyo sect was founded by Bunjiro in the nineteenth century. Bunjiro claimed to have special revelations to the effect that there is only one God. He believed that he was "possessed" by God, and revelations were uttered by him in this state concerning the Oneness and Goodness of the Deity.

Bunjiro became a Shinto priest although he repudiated superstitious practices. He taught the use of extempore prayer, "just as if you were talking to another human being". And he went beyond the narrow patriotism of his day to teach universal brotherhood. It is debated whether he had known Christian influence when his monotheistic teaching began. His sect claims to have three million followers and to have branches outside Japan, but it is not so serious a rival to Christianity as the next sect to be considered. Bunjiro said:

"No matter how thankfully one may read his rituals and make his purifications, if there is no sincerity within the heart it is the same as lying to God. The vain making of a big noise by the clapping of hands avails nothing, for even a little sound is heard by God. It is not necessary to speak in a loud voice or to practise intonations in prayer."[1]

A further sect, Tenri-kyo, "The Teaching of Divine Reason", was founded by a woman called Maekawa Miki. Her teachings on health and sickness are somewhat like those of Christian Science, faith-healing being the central part of the system. Maekawa Miki was a Buddhist of the Pure Land sect who was married to a Shinto husband. When she was forty years old she became "god-possessed", and under the force of the revelation she felt compelled to sell all the family property and give the money to the poor. She was persecuted and called a witch, but eventually she obtained recognition as founder of a new sect. Her revelations told her that evil and sickness were dust upon the soul, and rituals were used for purification. Dances, drummings, and incantations of psalms are used in the meetings, and the result of this excitement is to induce "god-possession". The sect claims over four million adherents and has missions outside Japan. It is believed that all the world will accept the revelation and be healed of its sickness. Miki said:

"When God appears and teaches you a matter completely,
Then the whole world is inspired with courage.
I am in haste to save you all and that right speedily.
So take courage, O hearts of all the world."[2]

This sect claims several million adherents and it rivals Christianity. The Shinto sects are helping to fill the vacuum caused by the decline of State Shinto, and are putting forth their claims to be the national religion of the non-Buddhist

[1] A. C. Bouquet, *Sacred Books of the World*, p. 325.
[2] Ibid., p. 326.

Japanese. It is, of course, not impossible that State Shinto may revive with the coming of more favourable conditions.

NOTE ON BUDDHISM IN THE PACIFIC ISLANDS

Buddhism has spread to many of the Pacific Islands and from there to North America. An important centre is in the Hawaiian Islands. Although the Hawaiians had their own native religion, and have now been largely christianized, yet there are many Japanese in the islands and they have spread Buddhism. It seems that many first-generation Japanese settlers have preserved a greater loyalty to Buddhism than that faith commands among many who have stayed in Japan. The strategic position of the islands between Asia and America makes them an important centre for Buddhist activity and missionary work.

The type of Buddhism here, of course, is of the Northern or Mahayana school, deriving from Japan. In Honolulu alone there are temples of the Jodo, Jodoshin, Shingon, Zen, and Nichiren sects. An International Buddhist Institute, linked with one in Japan, acts as a centre of propaganda.

An interesting feature of Buddhism in Hawaii is the use of European terms and the endeavour to make Buddhism acceptable to people of the West or of western education. At the opening of a new temple in 1953, there was a procession led by three hundred children of the "Sunday School", dressed in Japanese ceremonial robes and gold headdress, followed by twelve young men holding the white ropes attached to an ornate shrine on wheels, containing the image of Buddha Sakyamuni. These were followed by the "Archbishop" from Japan, the local "Bishop", Bhikshus (priests) and chanters with their bells and the regular choir. When they had entered the temple and performed the opening ceremony, verses were chanted for those who had died in the war, on the allied side and on the Japanese side. Then verses were sung for those who had contributed to the building of the temple but had passed away before its completion. The temple holds over six hundred people. Underneath there is an auditorium just as big for cinema shows and a stage for Japanese dances.

Services, called Hoji, in remembrance of the dead are observed by all sects. Beginning on the seventh day after death, the services are held every seven days until the forty-ninth. Then they are observed on the hundredth day, first year, third year, thirteenth, seventeenth, twenty-fifth, thirty-third, fiftieth, and hundredth years.

The extensive literature put out by the International Buddhist Institutes includes numerous statements of Buddhist doctrines with popular explanations for non-Buddhists, lives of the Buddha, and accounts of the special tenets of the Mahayana. The difference between Buddhist and other conceptions of God is explained in these terms:

"The eternal Buddha is impersonal yet contains all personality, he does not punish neither does he reward. Karma takes care of that. The Eternal Buddha is all mercy, all compassion, and is like the sun shining on the just and the unjust, on the good man and the bad man alike."[1]

Hymns and poems are composed in English, which remind one of Christian devotional verse:

"One morn in meditation
I watched the people throng
Around the blessed Teacher
As he slowly walked along . . .
And in His eyes reflected
I saw beyond, above,
The Face of the Lord Buddha,
Compassion, Light and Love."

There is no doubt that Mahayana Buddhism, like the Hinayana at the Sixth Buddhist Council, is awakening to feel that it has a wider world mission than hitherto, especially in leading the world into peace. Buddhist centres in America and Europe are very small, but the influence of their literature is much more considerable than the number of their adherents.

[1] E. S. Hunt, *Essentials and Symbols of the Buddhist Faith*, pp. 9, 14.

Short Bibliography

A. C. Underwood, *Shintoism* (Epworth)

E. V. Gatenby, *The Cloud-Men of Yamato* (Murray)

F. H. Smith, *The Buddhist Way of Life* (Hutchinson)

C. H. S. Ward, *Buddhism, Vol. 2. Mahayana* (Epworth)

C. Humphreys, *Buddhism* (Pelican)

A. Watts, *The Spirit of Zen* (Murray)

D. T. Suzuki, *Manual of Zen Buddhism* (Rider)

Epilogue

THIS short study of the religions of Asia has led us in bewildering variety into many lands. If it has served, in any way, to explode the fallacy that "all religions are the same", it will have done at least one good piece of work. It is the diversity of religion that is so astonishing. And this diversity may be found within the same all-embracing religion, such as Hinduism or Buddhism. Indeed so various are the different elements within Buddhism that we find a modern Buddhist questioning, of the Pure Land sect, "Is it Buddhism?"

With the study of the religions of Japan we have gone right to the other side of the world. And yet it has been seen that here is most deeply entrenched that religion of Buddhism which came from India, spread over the greater part of Asia, and claims to be a universal religion.

The phenomenon of a universal religion is an important one, and it is not so common as is often thought. Indeed, a universal and missionary religion is a rare and late development. If you are not born an Indian or a Japanese you can scarcely be a Hindu or a Shintoist. You can hardly follow the .Jewish faith unless you are a Jew by birth. Only by breaking free from Judaism did Christianity become a world religion.

Islam is a universal missionary religion also, but it is a late-comer on the scene of religion and it borrowed its world-view, partly at least, from Christianity. That does not make it any less significant as a claimant for the allegiance of mankind.

Buddhism in Asia, Islam in Asia and Africa, Christianity in Europe and America and elsewhere, are international faiths. In the last century Christianity has made tremendous strides, into practically every country in the world, and has become truly world-wide. Professor Latourette has said that in this century Christianity has spread further and increased more in numbers than at any similar period during the two thousand years of her history. Buddhism and Islam are also awakening slowly to send missionary propaganda into the western lands. There is a great struggle on for the soul of the world. At least this does reveal the virility of religion in the world to-day.

Throughout this study we have tried to remain impartial and objective, and we do not intend to make a reasoned statement of faith here or to offer a snap judgement. We have preferred to let the facts speak for themselves. It was a Muslim mystic who said, "The lamps are different, but the Light is the same." Some of the lamps have become obscure and give little light; others shine with varying radiance. But there is One True Light "which lighteth every man".

Index

137